360° OF SUCCESS

360° OF SUCCESS

Money • Relationships • Energy°Time:
The 4 Essential Ingredients to Create
Professional and Personal Success in Your Life?

From the introduction until the end this is a power house book! Packed full of the "how tos" when it comes to personal excellence and success in life, Ana equips the reader with practical application guidance that gives birth to results: emotionally, physically, and spiritually. Because Ana writes like she speaks, this read is like a face-to-face conversation that unfolds with ease, enthusiasm and grace. Ana has created laser focus around the 4 essential ingredients that fuel personal greatness along with the necessary wisdom to make it all happen.

Lauren E Miller
Founder of Stress Solutions University.com
International Speaker/Author

You'll love reading Ana Weber's book, <u>360 Degrees of Success: Money-Relationships-Energy-Time! The 4 Essential Ingredients to Create Personal and Professional Success in Your Life</u>. She believes life is full of possibility, and you can't help but feel her warm and radiant spirit as you connect with her writing. Blessed with an uplifting way of looking at life, Ana shares how to solve problems and attract everything you need by changing your attitude and applying the simple philosophies of passion, priority, and portion in your daily life. In simple and practical ways, Ana shows you how to attract more money, improve your relationships, spark your energy, and rid yourself of time busters. Then, she links them all together! Ana is a great mentor, and her story will inspire you to go beyond the ordinary to the extraordinary. She is compelling to the core and makes strangers into friends in less time than it takes to make a cup of coffee. There's more than one lesson in each of her chapters, so drink it all in, one sip at a time!

Robin Samora, Founder www.RobinSamoraInc.com
Creating Fresh and Engaging Strategies
that Get You Noticed as an Expert

360°
OF SUCCESS

MONEY • RELATIONSHIPS • ENERGY • TIME

*the 4 essential ingredients to create personal
and professional success in your life*

ANA WEBER

NEW YORK

360° OF SUCCESS

*Money, Relationships, Energy, Time: The 4 Essential Ingredients
to Create Personal and Professional Success in Your Life*

Published in New York, New York, by Morgan James Publishing. Morgan James and
The Entrepreneurial Publisher are trademarks of Morgan James, LLC.
www.MorganJamesPublishing.com

The Morgan James Speakers Group can bring authors to your live event. For more
information or to book an event visit The Morgan James Speakers Group at
www.TheMorganJamesSpeakersGroup.com.

ISBN 978-1-61448-910-8 paperback
ISBN 978-1-61448-913-9 hard cover
ISBN 978-1-61448-911-5 eBook
Library of Congress Control Number:
2013948909

FREE eBook edition for your
existing eReader with purchase

PRINT NAME ABOVE

For more information,
instructions, restrictions, and
to register your copy, go to
www.bitlit.ca/readers/register
or use your QR Reader to scan
the barcode:

Cover Design by:
Rachel Lopez
www.r2cdesign.com

Interior Design by:
Bonnie Bushman
bonnie@caboodlegraphics.com

In an effort to support local communities, raise awareness and funds, Morgan James Publishing
donates a percentage of all book sales for the life of each book to Habitat for Humanity Peninsula
and Greater Williamsburg.

Get involved today, visit
www.MorganJamesBuilds.com.

**Habitat
for Humanity®**
Peninsula and
Greater Williamsburg
Building Partner

DEDICATION

To my family I love and cherish and so proud of:
My Mother Erzsebeth, my husband Mario, my
son Sean, daughter-in-law Sarah, and my two
grandchildren: Logan, and Mia.

CONTENTS

FOREWORD

Last spring, I met Ana Weber and her engaging husband, Mario Haber, for brunch on a sunny day in downtown Palo Alto, California. Ana had interviewed me about my book, *Branding Pays*, for her blog earlier in the year. During our interview, we were delighted to find that we both had farming roots, spoke French, and shared the same optimistic view on life. When Ana and Mario had occasion to visit the Bay Area, it was natural for her to reach out to me.

Ana was ebullient, funny, and a great storyteller. I was amazed to hear how she went from being a penniless immigrant to growing business after business exponentially only to lose her fortune in a bad series of events.

Ana started over after moving to Israel from Romania as a child. When she arrived in Israel, she did not know the language and had to live in a dormitory for poor and orphaned children, because her mother lacked the money to raise her. Ana has started over so many times, including when she lost her home and savings, that she could be the poster child for resilience. After meeting Ana, I thought, "If only we could bottle and share her positive energy, the world would be a better place."

Today we have the next best thing. Ana has captured the wisdom from her life and career in her book, 360 Degrees of Success *Money-Relationships-Time-Energy! The Four Essential Ingredients to Create Professional and Personal Success in Your Life.*

She applies her 3 P's of Passion, Portion, and Priority to these essential ingredients in a way that is practical and actionable. As a bonus, she sometimes adds Preparation as a fourth P.

Money, relationships, time, and energy are intertwined. I love the fact that Ana, as a 360° business and personal coach, integrates these ingredients into her consulting and this book.

If we all followed Ana's advice, we would lead happier, healthier lives where our money would grow along with our relationships. Thank you, Ana, for showing us the way.

Karen Kang
Corporate and Personal Branding Strategist
Author of *Branding Pays: The Five-Step System
to Reinvent Your Personal Brand*

ACKNOWLEDGMENTS

My gratitude to Scott Frishman for spending quality time with me and giving me the best advice ever. You are a man of great wisdom and poise.

My sincere thanks to Kelly Jo Eldredge for helping me pull it all together in record time.

To Steve Harrison, Marc Goodman, Matthew Bennett, Mellanie True Hills, Dr. Elizabeth Lombardo, Dan Janal, Jamie Bright Forman, Julia and Doug Salisbury, Marcia and Ted Reece, Judith and Igal Rochverger, Michelle and Andrew Malatskey, Klara and Nissan Zysman, Zev and Olga Zysman, Tzipi and Stuart Kricun Caroline Shrednick, Eve and Bob Soltz, Helena and Richard Stoltz, Boaz Rauchwerger Kay and Zvika Hartman, Yona and David Goldberg, Shoshana and Avi Ben-Hur, Shalom and Mika Nesher, Gila and Shmuel Kotlovsky and Chen and Idan Kotlovsky, Carmela and Avaram Ben-Hur, Olivia and Tim Tran, Renee Elle, Tin and Pourie Parsai, Genia, Erika Weinstein, Dorit and Don Weiss, Romy and David Siegel, Elizabeth Gordon,

Francis and Sabrina Hsu, Rena and Batya Lahav, and Alex Bayer. And to my extended family: Elsa, Enrique, Gladys, Sylvia, Mark, Matthew, Sharon, Vanessa, Michael, Aaron, Derrek, Jennifer and Amanda. Thank you so much, Chase, for working on my new website and programs.

INTRODUCTION

Presently I am embracing the challenges of four careers. I am a 360° business and personal coach; I lead motivational speaking programs, and maintain an active blog. In addition, I work as a freelance journalist and have written numerous books and articles focusing on the importance of developing passion and confidence in all aspects of life.

On the personal side, I am a wife and mother who cherish the art of cooking and preparing daily meals for my family; including my beloved mother who I financially and emotionally support. For daily relaxation I engage in long walks on Balboa Island where I embrace the beach's calm ambiance.

I enjoy the adventure of traveling with my family. I find this an excellent way to spend quality time and strengthen my relationships with my son, daughter-in-law and grandchildren. Once a year, I take the grandchildren on a short getaway, usually to the Hotel del Coronado on Coronado Island, California. We love it there, and the place has grown on us over the years—the beach, the pools, the sand, the greenery, the good food, and listening to great bands while we enjoy hamburgers and ice cream. In this one spot we connect and share the special moments of life's simple splendor.

On a recent trip to New York to attend the BEA (Book Expo America); I was boarding the plane with my usual big smile, when one of the flight attendants made a lovely remark as she greeted me. "I love it when I see people with a great attitude entering the plane," she said. "Welcome aboard!"

Later during the flight, the flight attendant and I started talking. She asked me the same questions others have asked: "Were you always like this—friendly, smiling, and full of energy and spunk? You have a magnetic personality. I want to know more about you. What you do?"

When people get to know me better, they tend to ask another set of questions: "How do you accomplish so much? What is your secret? How can I apply it to my life? I would love to be in your shoes!"

Indeed, today I am an extremely happy and content individual. I embrace everything I do, and I practice what I teach and write about 24/7. My answer is simple. I enjoy and fully activate

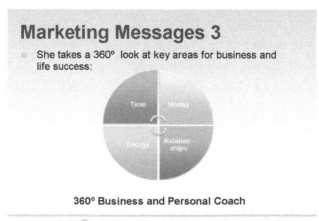

Marketing Messages 3

She takes a 360° look at key areas for business and life success:

Time | Money
Energy | Relationships

360° Business and Personal Coach

the four essential ingredients we cannot live without: **money**, **relationships**, **energy**, and **time**.

Is there anything else out there?

I have decided to spread the message and share my secrets and wisdom with the world. When people ask me what I do my response is quick and simple: "I help people reignite their passion for life!"

That's it.

I wasn't born this way—outgoing, friendly, humble, confident, and entirely filled with freedom and passion. I grew up an only child in Romania, and was the absolute opposite—shy, insecure, unfriendly, and totally isolated.

People have difficulty believing this, but so it was.

I was a sad little girl, rarely smiling and taking life far too seriously. My childhood wasn't easy. I recognized the fact that things had to change, but the ability to change felt scary and utterly out of reach.

My life took a dramatic turn with the birth of my son. I was a young, twenty-year-old mother, but I instinctively began to build a loving and giving relationship with him. My overwhelming love for my son brought me out of my shell. I became friendlier and more confident as time went on, and I realized I also felt happier and more fulfilled.

Gradually, I began tapping into my passion seed for life. I began to realize I had a purpose, and I was willing to grow into it. I took small steps and learned through my work and personal life how to love, share, give, and receive as I juggled my new life. To my surprise, the more I practiced implementing the four essential ingredients, the better life became.

Fast forward to today. I have spent a lifetime developing practical and friendly tools that link the four ingredients. I have discovered the ingredients of money, relationships, energy, and time build on one another—if one is absent, the rest will f all apart.

The simple truth is I learned to love everything I do. I realized that the things I don't enjoy are actually connecting ribbons for everything I profoundly value. They tie me to my passions.

For example: I don't like to do dishes. However, I know why a home-cooked meal is so valuable—the energy I receive; the fuel for better focus; a good night's sleep; and a healthy, positive attitude. Plus, I love to cook! Now I see that doing the dishes connects me to my passion and a healthier, happier me. It doesn't seem such a terrible chore after all!

I shared a bit of my personal story. Now, it's your turn. What is your WHY? What is your personal story?

Whether you are a young student just graduating from college embarking on a new life, a dynamic corporate executive, or an entrepreneur establishing your first business, this book is for you. We all must find a way to utilize the four essential ingredients of money, relationships, energy, and time to live a full and satisfying life.

Once you read this book and have an opportunity to put the materials into practice, and you will recognize how to build the life you desire. Personal and professional abundance is within your reach!

In addition to the four essential ingredients, you will also activate the three powerful P formulas:

1. **Passion**
2. **Portion**
3. **Priority**

Most importantly, please know this book will help you tremendously when life challenges come your way. We are all human. We will make mistakes throughout our lives. We will overlook important things. We will have unrealistic expectations. But when we utilize the comprehensive tools provided in this book, we will build the bridges of our success. Each time we cross a bridge; we will breathe in the newness of life.

Our journey will not be perfect. I have experienced disappointments and let downs along the way. I still have dreams that I am working to materialize. But I learned to trust this process. I treasure my journey. I live in the now with a purpose for tomorrow. That purpose imbues me with emotional and physical strength and stability. I appreciate the power of the four essential ingredients, and I pray with gratitude the opportunity to share the wisdom I have been granted.

Let these pages be your guide. Keep the book handy and re-read chapters when life presents challenges and you want additional guidance. Bring the tools into action each and every day, and you will learn to shift your attitude and reignite your passion. Soon, you will have a huge smile on your face. You will take care of yourself, and be instrumental in supporting others along the way. Are you ready to jump into life and get a 360° view of the possibilities it offers?

So our journey begins… Let's pursue a happy life together!
Ana

PART I

MONEY—MASTER OR SERVANT?

Money. Does the word make you panic? Is it a commodity based on fear, or is it a positive tool in your life?

This book is the sequel to my book *The Money Flow: How to Make Money your Friend and Ally, Have a Great Life, and Improve the World*. In *The Money Flow*, in my preceding book I examined the aspects that influence our personal relationships with money. Now let's take those ideas a step further to develop our comprehensive 360° view.

Is money your master or your servant? It's a valuable question. Let's learn to take control of money and initiate its circulation, so that it benefits us and our world.

STARTING WITH THE THREE P'S

ooooooooooooooooooooooooooooooooooooooooooo

At a young age I learned that money was a source of stress. I needed to modify my outlook on money and make it my partner rather than adversary; or I simply would not survive. So I chose to make friends with money.

I found that attitude was everything, and when I changed my attitude toward money, doors opened to me that I could not fathom as a small girl working alongside my mom in the kiosk in Romania, or as a student living with other poor children and orphans in a Kibbutz Mossad.

Happiness is closely related to your relationship with money. It is important, when establishing a positive alliance with money, to realize that money as a stand-alone commodity will not create contentment. The power is in your *relationship* with money.

Maintaining a friendship with money is simply building a healthy relationship. We spend time building relationships with family members, friends, coworkers, neighbors, children, and spouses, but we never consider spending time cultivating a relationship with money. The following information will guide you in pursuing and nourishing a positive relationship with money that will last a lifetime.

I will set a foundation for your relationship by sharing the three P's that helped me sustain a healthy association with money. At first you may feel these three words don't apply to money, but you will soon recognize they are the source of an abundant financial life.

The three P's are:

1. **Passion**
2. **Priority**
3. **Portion**

Passion

Passion is powerful. It changes negative motivation to positive motivation. Passion is the seed that ignites your spirit and fuels your desire to live a fulfilling life. Life without passion is dull and meaningless, basically existence. But with passion, it is boundless! The sky is the limit!

Passion provides you the additional energy needed to overcome the challenges you face. It leads directly to a happy, content, and unique life. It is the seed that will feed your soul, and when it blossoms, you will truly know what it is to live.

When you identify your passion in life, focus your energy in that direction. The money flow will follow when you give your passion the time it deserves.

People often tell me they wish they could bottle my energy. I frequently have a big smile on my face and a sparkle underneath the surface. That zing of energy comes from passion. I found my passion, and I nurture and cherish it every day.

What is your passion? Are you giving it the attention it deserves?

Priority

When you begin to nourish your passion seed, you become strongly motivated to do only those things that fill the passion category. However, in the real world there are additional duties that you are obligated to fulfill. Developing a healthy sense of Priority is the next step in organizing your life and making it receptive to a positive money flow.

There are 1,440 minutes in a day, but they quickly slip away when you don't take time to prioritize. Priority allows you to get a handle on balancing the things you want to do with the things you need to do.

The meaning of priority is the sense that one thing is more important than another. It is imperative that you look deeper to understand this concept. Priority is a tool that helps you control time with respect to activities that shift time from before to now. Ultimately, priority is realizing and responding to the activities that shift time.

Priority allows you to stay in the now. You are able to concentrate on the activity you have given priority, because you have recognized that it requires your primary attention.

When you stay in the present with an activity, you will accomplish it more efficiently than thinking about the next item. Priority imparts focus. It shows you how to become more proficient in completing tasks; thereby freeing up time to pursue your passion.

Portion

Portion is a part of a whole. It is also a useful tool in distributing your prioritized activities over the 1,440 minutes in a day. Time is money.

You become more adept at portioning when you learn to apportion. What does that mean? Apportion means to distribute according to a plan or set apart for a special purpose. The main phrase is *according to a plan*. It is not random. Planning allows you to allocate time portions according to the priority of the activity and the actual amount of time it takes to complete it.

Activities can be categorized into three areas with respect to time portion:

1. Casual
2. Planned
3. Unplanned

Casual activities are performed when an opportunity comes along, and completing the activity will not compromise a higher priority activity. A great example of this is stopping by the store for milk on the way home from work. You need milk. The opportunity comes along when you drive by the grocery store. It will only take an extra five minutes, and you are able to cross the task off your list. It is more efficient than going home and then back out again to make a special trip to the store.

Planned activities are performed when you set aside a portion of time prior to conducting the activity. You plan for it; you put it on the schedule. For example, you may know that it takes you an hour to write up a proposal for a client, and it is due the next day. You schedule time on your calendar to complete the task.

When you get to the time you have portioned, the proposal is your priority for that hour.

Unplanned activities are those that pop up and suddenly become your highest priority. Unplanned activities grab their own portion, which acquire the time portions you have committed to other activities. An example of an unplanned activity is a medical emergency. It immediately becomes your top priority and reserves whatever portion of the time you need until it can be resolved.

Portion is extremely important. Always divide your day into smaller portions of time in order to see your activities through to completion. It is easier to manage one-hour or two-hour portions than to struggle to wrap your mind around what to do for 1,440 minutes.

Things do not always go according to plan, so you learn to create additional time portions by adding casual activities to planned activities—also known as multitasking. The better you get at portioning your time, the more you will discover extra minutes to pursue your passion. You will find numerous ways to portion your time. You can become a master of arranging these chunks of minutes so you have time to enjoy life. This balance and flow promotes the development of your life's passion.

The three P's are all about balance. They provide the tools you need to take control of your life. You do not need to be a slave to money, and you do not need to enslave it to make it work for you. That is not the relationship you're seeking. What you are developing is a relationship that enables you to understand and respect the importance of money and where it belongs throughout the course of your life.

When you take a look at your day-to-day life and get in touch with your Passion, Priorities, and Portion, you will develop a creative relationship with money that initiates a positive flow throughout everything you do. It becomes a simple giving and receiving motion—when, why, where, and what portion of your money is being spent or saved. That is the dance.

Perfecting this dance and filtering your relationship through a positive attitude will create a successful relationship with money—no intimidation, no fear, no judgment, no anger. You will drop bad habits from your former relationship with money and pursue a stronger partnership.

Passion, Priority, and Portion—these three P's have anchored my success. Observe how you balance them each and every day.

JUST TEN MINUTES A DAY?
THE 3-STEP/30 DAY PROGRAM

oooooooooooooooooooooooooooooooooooooooo

Now, let's continue to build on the three P's and expand our view. Our next tool is the **3-Step/30-Day Program** that I developed to incorporate the three P's into my life. Don't be concerned that a 30-day program seems like a lot of work. This only takes ten minutes a day! I have streamlined the process for you to make it simple.

Relax and enjoy this process! Don't worry about whether or not you're doing it right or if you're deriving the best results as you go along. Remain in the now, and you will discover the answers you seek.

It took me about eight years to develop and perfect this process. I began by using myself as the guinea pig, trying various routes and adjusting them along the way. I then offered the system to my coaching clients, and they appreciated the results the program provided—especially because they saw a significant change in their lives in only ten minutes a day.

You don't have ten minutes to spare? I don't believe you! Everyone can find an extra ten minutes in their day. Set your alarm ten minutes early; return from your lunch break ahead of time; enjoy the experience of these exercises for just ten minutes after the family has gone to bed. It's only ten minutes. You can do it.

Each step is repeated for 10 days, so you have plenty of time to get the most out of the activity. You carry out the first 10-minute activity on days 1-10, the second activity on days 11-20, and the last activity on days 21-30. Make sense? Each activity builds on the previous activity. Do not over think the process. Just do it.

The power of the 3-Step/30-Day Program comes from its simplicity. If someone told you that you could significantly change your life by devoting only ten minutes a day to a simple exercise, wouldn't you give it a shot? Okay, so here we go....

Step 1: The First 10 Days

This is a challenging one. Are you ready?

Take 10 minutes—at the same time every day for 10 days—and do ABSOLUTELY NOTHING! Do not skip this step, even if you don't believe you need it. Give it a chance!

The Benefit

It sounds counterintuitive, but the benefits of doing nothing are spectacular. When you do absolutely nothing for 10 minutes, on 10 consecutive days, you will begin to de-clutter your thoughts and rejuvenate your spirit. It will recharge your batteries with clarity and new energy. Doing nothing will help you say goodbye to stress, worry, and fear.

As gardener must clear weeds to make room for the garden to grow, de-cluttering your mind will create space for your passion seed to flourish. We all possess the passion seed, but that seed has to grow before we can truly see it, feel it, and make it a part of our core. Ten minutes of quiet nurtures that passion seed; it fertilizes it, removes the weeds and generates room for your passion to grow.

You may think doing nothing doesn't require instruction. You're right—but it does require the right mindset. Accordingly, here are some guidelines I have found helpful:

Sit in a comfortable chair, in a room or relaxing outdoor space and wear comfortable clothing.

Turn off the TV, computer, radio, music player, phone and other sources of interruption.

Stare at a nondescript object. You can close your eyes (as long as you don't nod off).

Observe the thoughts that stream through your mind and let them go.

After 10 days of doing nothing for 10 minutes each day, you are ready for Step 2.

Step 2: The Second 10 Days

Once again, set aside the same 10 minutes every day for each of the second 10 days. This time, write down three things you desire to incorporate into your life. They can be ideas, material things, and goals, whatever you choose to bring into your life that day. Ponder your list for 10 minutes. What are your thoughts? How do you feel when you think about them? Make a fresh list every day. It can have the same three things on it as the day before, or you can replace any or all of them, as long as you always have three on your list.

The Benefit

The three things you desire, write down, and then contemplate will reflect and reinforce your growing passion seed. As you continue to write, think and feel some items will fall by the wayside, replaced by others. Note the items that you delete from the list. They are still important to you, but their priority is lower than the things that replaced them.

At the end of the 10 days, you will have three solid desires that truly reflect your passion. Ten minutes of contemplation and reflection on the things you want in your life each day will lead you to increased enthusiasm and determination—and ultimately, greater happiness and improved money flow.

Step 3: The Third 10 Days

You've been cultivating these three things for 10 days. Now you are ready to bring them into your life. Take the same 10 minutes every day for each of the third 10 days to TAKE ACTION on your three goals. Make specific plans to turn them into reality. Start with broad outlines on the first day, and work toward step-by-step details as the 10 days progresses. Correct and adjust your plans, as you to fill in the details.

Note: You may be tempted to go directly to Step 3. Don't! By going through the whole 3-step process and utilizing the entire 30 days, you will articulate your true passion seed more deeply and clearly. When you move into action, that action is apt to create permanent, positive change. Why? Because you have been actively warming up and training your brain. Now your powerful mind (and mindset) is ready to for you to meet those deep inner desires.

The Benefit

At the end of the third 10 days, you will have a workable plan to bring three things you're passionate about into your life. You'll be ready, eager, and determined to incorporate those plans into reality by acting on them one step at a time.

By this time, you will begin to see results. Money and time will start to work for you, and you will be prepared to portion their forward flow.

Portioning Worksheets

Remember the third P? It was **Portion**. The way to activate the action plan you created in the 3-step/30 Day Program is to divide your day into smaller pieces and assign tasks or goals to each portion. I call this "portioning." Plan to portion the 1,440 minutes of each day so part of the day reflects your passions and priorities, thereby reinforcing the goals you identified in the 30 day program. The Portioning Worksheets will help you focus on the NOW. They will guide you in finding and nourishing your passion seed by clarifying your priorities.

Most of us have planners to schedule our time. Yet, most of us don't accomplish everything that we enter into our planners. Why do you think that is? It is because they don't reflect our passion and priority. Your Portioning Worksheets don't replace your planners, but they will help you consider how your activities can advance your passions and priorities *before* you enter them in your planner. The worksheets offer you further feedback by allowing you to reflect on the activities you actually perform.

The worksheets I will show you next may be requested by emailing me at ana360degreecoach@gmail.com, or you can photocopy the following pages. It's also beneficial to download the worksheets, since you have a fresh list every day and can carry over unfinished items without retyping.

Portioning Your Month

When you portion your month, list the activities you expect to accomplish and assign a priority to each. Use any priority ranking that works for you. For me, I find a scale of 1 (highest priority) to 5 (lowest priority) works well. It's perfectly fine to assign the same priority status to multiple activities.

Include activities you *must* do and the activities you *choose* to do. After completing the list, identify the month and year for future reference. You may find it helpful to retain the completed worksheets so you can refer to them whenever you want; as well as chart your progress. After a few years, you will be amazed by your ability to embrace and achieve larger passions.

Each Monthly Activities Worksheet is similar to a chapter heading in a book. The weekly sheets are subsections; and the daily accomplishment logs round out the chapter. Your binder might look something like this:

April
    Week One
        Day One
        Day Two
        Day Three
        Day Four
        Day Five
        Day Six
        Day Seven

Week Two
    Day One
    Day Two
    Day Three
    Day Four
    Day Five
    Day Six
    Day Seven
Week Three
    Day One
    Day Two
    Day Three
    Day Four
    Day Five
    Day Six
    Day Seven
Week Four
    Day One
    Day Two
    Day Three
    Day Four
    Day Five
    Day Six
    Day Seven
May
Week One
    Day One
    Day Two
    Day Three
    Day Four

Day Five
Day Six
Day Seven
Week Two
Day One
Day Two
Day Three
Day Four
Day Five
Day Six
Day Seven
Week Three
Day One
Day Two
Day Three
Day Four
Day Five
Day Six
Day Seven
Week Four
Day One
Day Two
Day Three
Day Four
Day Five
Day Six
Day Seven

Draw on your Monthly Activities Worksheet to complete entries in your planner. This worksheet gives you the big picture. It allows you to consider *what*, instead of just *when*, and that lets you find time to work on important or crucial tasks. If you only utilize a planner, and only focus on the *when*, you could become easily bogged down in things that seem urgent but are not critical. In addition, you could neglect to make time for important things. This system ensures the important steps you need to achieve your deepest goals are met.

You can include activities for the next month, BUT be clear that they do not have priority for the current month. I assign a priority of 0 to future activities.

Here's a sample Monthly Activities Worksheet:

Monthly Activities		
Want To Do		Priority

Need To Do		Priority	
Month/Year			

Portioning Each Week

Now, portion your weeks. Write the start date on the sheet, list the activities you want to accomplish, and *assign a day and length of time you'll work on each activity*. So you don't get overwhelmed, only include the activities you intend to do this week, even if you have other to-do items on your Monthly Activities Worksheet. Now, transfer these tasks to your planner. This guarantees that you allocate time to accomplish your most important priorities. Here's a sample Weekly Activities Worksheet:

Weekly Activities	Day(s)

Beginning Date for Week	

Portioning Your Days

Portioning your months and weeks is a looking-ahead activity. But when you portion your days, you have to look back. Your Daily Activities Worksheet helps you fine-tune your planning based on what you actually completed. Unlike the monthly and weekly worksheets, you don't use it to fill in your planner or calendar. Instead, you check to see how well your plan is working.

Date the sheet and list each activity you performed during the day along with notes about whether you had allocated sufficient time.

Here's a sample Daily Activities Worksheet:

Daily Activities	Timing / Effectiveness

Day/Date	

Congratulations! By completing the 3-Step/30-Day Program and the Portioning Worksheets, you're already preparing to make friends with money and experience a positive money flow. You're cultivating fertile ground to nurture and grow your passion seed and creating space in your life to accomplish your deepest hopes and desires.

GETTING INTO THE FLOW

oooooooooooooooooooooooooooooooooo

We've learned some excellent tools to draw out our passions and pay closer attention to how we spend our time. After all, time is money. It's also true we tend to spend more time and work harder to accomplish the goals we are passionate about. We have a lot working for us at this moment. Now, we will use this information to develop a full 360° of success.

The word *flow* is the key. When money starts to flow, it has an opportunity to grow. You want your money to grow. To accomplish this you must put it into play. Money must circulate. It is the only way we truly develop a relationship with it. When we circulate money, we become the masters of our relationship with it. We are in control.

This cycle is also crucial for our global economy. For example, when you decide to take a vacation to recharge and rejuvenate your life, you purchase airline tickets, pay for accommodations, buy meals, and purchase gifts during your stay. By doing this you boost local economies in the places you visit. When money circulates, everyone benefits.

Unhealthy relationships with money breed fear and insecurity. This often causes people to stop circulating money. This inactivity is dangerous, in that it halts the give-and-take that allows us to thrive. Don't hold too tightly to money. When you stop circulating money, the entire system stagnates. Money *flow* is the key to success, not money hold.

I'm not suggesting that you run out and spend all your money in order to be successful. Excess is equally unhealthy. Moderation and stability are the key elements to achieving financial success. Examine your ratio of income, expenses, and obligations and make sure it's a healthy balance. Nurture the health of your money flow, and you will see your wealth grow.

It is difficult for a business to grow if its leaders are unwilling to spend money on supplies, employees, marketing, development, and other important factors. Get your money into play. Let it flow, and expect healthy results.

The secret to creating positive money flow is to appreciate money. Respect it and understand what it can do for you. But understand that money does not own you! You're free to live your life however you choose. Money is neither your master nor your slave; it's your friend.

Money flow will continuously be an integral part of your personal and business finances; that's why it is a powerful ally. It's a tool for your financial strength and freedom.

Planning is important. When you pay attention to the projected expenses and income that create your personal money flow, you are able to control how, where, and when your money will flow. If you work on salary, you know exactly how much money you'll have in your bank account each month, and can easily set a budget, put money aside to invest and save, and manage long-term planning.

While planning is simpler if you have a salary or other fixed income, the rewards are often greater when you're an entrepreneur. When you have your own business, money flow is influenced by six major components:

1. Quality products or services—including excellent customer service
2. Market demand
3. On-time delivery
4. Trust based relationships
5. Equitable methods of payment, discounts, and credit terms
6. Accurate and efficient maintenance of paperwork

When you work with vendors and customers, these suggestions will strengthen your cash flow:

- Honor your commitments
- Negotiate terms that are fair to everyone
- Pay with credit cards to buy more time. Pay the cards in full before the due date
- Pay early when it entitles you to discounts

Once you learn to maintain a healthy money flow, you will never run out of cash. You will be able to purchase items as you need them, and you won't worry about debt. It's a powerful feeling to be in control of your financial health.

But don't get too obsessed with money! There are enough Scrooges in the world. If you want to experience complete contentment, happiness, and freedom, make certain you're also cultivating the other things that make you happy.

Avoid the trap of workaholism. Reserve time to pursue your passions, take a day off and play with your children or grandchildren, plan a special getaway with your life partner, or exercise; nurture the parts of your life that boost your happiness.

Passive Income

When you create passive or residual income streams, you earn more while working less. Instead of being paid once for your time, you are continuously paid for the value you've already provided. Examples include:

- Investment income (interest and dividends)
- Royalties from a book you wrote or music you've recorded
- Sales from products you created or financed
- Rental income

Passive income streams remove the direct need to constantly create money flow, thereby freeing your time for other pursuits.

Building a healthy lifestyle and success with money relies on one thing: YOU. You must be authentic in all of your pursuits. Build your reputation on integrity, quality, accuracy, and dedication. Embrace each challenge with a problem-solving attitude. Build real relationships and demonstrate genuine interest in others. When you live your life in this manner you'll discover people will reciprocate in kind.

You are the creator of your chosen lifestyle. Please use these tools to their full advantage on your path to a wonderful and engaging life.

IT'S DEEP

ooooooooooo

Each year I deepen my relationship with money. I actively participate in money flow in my business and my personal life, and I recognize it is a delicate balance. It's a relationship, and there is continuous give and take. I found out the hard way how important it is to stay within my means, while overcoming my fear of not having enough money. I had to stop craving more and decide that I was satisfied with what I had. It was a difficult process, but I learned how to create a healthy relationship with money.

You can build your relationship with money by developing the three P's; nurturing your passion seed through the 3-step/30-day program; and making sure you always have an accurate account of your business and personal finances. Do not guess. Take an objective look at your financial situation on a regular basis. This alleviates fear and allows you to make adjustments. Sometimes you have to work harder for your money or make other plans to maintain a healthy relationship with this new friend. Other times, the money flow seems easy, like spending time with an old pal.

You will successfully navigate the ups and downs of your relationship with money if you honor and respect it. When money circulates, trust and maturity enter the relationship.

When your children leave for college, you still love them and think about them and wish them the best—but you no longer see them daily. You might get an occasional text, email, or phone call, but you have to trust that they are doing the right things and leading productive, happy, healthy lives. The same holds true when you let money circulate. You may decide to invest it and for a while, your money flow decreases. But you trust that you have maintained a healthy relationship with it and the end result will ultimately be fruitful. Money is your friend for life. It will flow back to you if you continue to cultivate a positive relationship with it.

Remember: Like any healthy relationship, positive money flow begins with a positive attitude. Because I desire a great relationship with money, I spend time cultivating it. Money helps fulfill my dreams; it has become a strong ally. You will become friends with money, if you take these tips and lessons to heart.

BUT IT DOESN'T MAKE YOU HAPPY

ooooooooooooooooooooooooooooooooooooooooooooooooo

Having money is only one ingredient of success. It is not the means to a happy life. Money doesn't make you happy. It's a tool. Many people around the world are happy even when their bank accounts are slim.

A happy life is built on surrounding yourself with people who love you, maintaining physical health, pursuing your passions, and taking time to relax and unwind; the things that spice up your life and add flavor to your days.

Let's move on to the next important ingredient for a complete 360° perspective of happiness and success: Relationships.

PART II

RELATIONSHIPS—
WE ARE NOT ISLANDS

Relationships are tricky. We strive for healthy and fruitful relationships, but we often take actions that sabotage them. We long to connect, and as soon as we do, we can't wait to be left alone. If we follow our first emotional impulse, we will never develop stable relationships.

So what should we do?

Let's start off with the first rule of relationships:

Be more interested.
Be less interesting!

What does that mean to you?

We are all attention seekers. We love to be heard and have the opportunity to express ourselves.

I challenge you to turn around this human need and regard it from the other side. How can you take a new approach? Rather than display how interesting you are at every opportunity, introduce the power of being interested in the value of others. Discover who they are, what makes them tick, where their passions lie. When you change your focus, you contribute immediately to building relationships.

Whether you are on the phone, communicating via email, or speaking in person, practice turning the focus to the other person, help them feel open and free to be heard. Give them room to share what's on their mind.

Relationships have a profound impact on our lives. They directly impact business success, health, personal happiness, and many other areas of our lives. Did you know successful relationships reduce stress? We feel less overwhelmed when we actively participate in healthy relationships.

Here is an everyday example of how you can become more interested and less interesting:

Example

You receive a referral from a friend for a potential new client. What do you do?

1. Email the person: Dear John D... I'm glad Fred introduced the two of us... I am happy to meet you... Looking forward to hearing from you... I believe we could be of great support to each other.
2. Wait! Give the person time to respond.

3. If you receive a prompt response, pick up the phone and say hello: Hi this is Ana W... How are you today? Thanks so much for your email (or phone message).

At this point, you are ready to introduce the three secret formulas for creating a relationship. These formulas are incredibly valuable; because they help you change the focus to the other person thereby increasing the power of your relationships.

The three secret formulas for creating a relationship consist of three questions:

1. Where are you from?
2. What line of work are you in?
3. What is your passion?

Let's revisit our example. You are on the phone with John D. You've made contact, now is your opportunity to deepen the relationship by incorporating the three secret formulas.

"So, John, where are you from?"

Wait for John to share his background. Give him time to share.

"How long have you been in this line of work?"

By asking these questions you demonstrate your interest. Listen to him share additional information about his work and interests. Pay close attention and ask follow-up questions.

"What is your passion, John?"

This question surprises people, but they love to answer it. Unfortunately, many people never consider this question. It reveals so much about a person For example, John might share his hobby, his long-time dream, a goal in life, or a project he is working on.

You will get the inside scoop on John if you ask this question and take genuine interest in his reply.

Why do you think these three secret formulas are so valuable? Their value is in their simplicity.

The secret formulas work for three reasons. First they signify a genuine interest in the other person. It's surprising how seldom this happens and how greatly it is appreciated.

Secondly, they provide you history and perspective. When you know about the other person, you have a clearer understanding of ways in which you may connect and assist each other. When they discuss their line of work, you learn about their stability, dedication to their business, the amount of time they've spent in a particular career, and if they are looking for a change.

Finally, when you prompt a person to share their passion, you ascertain what truly makes them tick. You might discover compatible interests. For example, maybe you both enjoy traveling abroad. This opens the door to creating a more meaningful relationship.

Most importantly, when you pose these questions, you ignite a spark in that individual. They may have lost their passion as they dealt with life's challenges, or they have a new passion they can't wait to share, but no one asks. Either way, people love to answer questions related to their past experiences; their current path; or their future dreams, goals, visions, and ideas. This empowers them to feel creative and engaged in life. Give them the opportunity to share their thoughts. It's an amazing gift.

The beauty of the three secret formulas is they provide a wealth of information about the person you are getting to know, and connect you in three time zones:

- Past
- Present
- Future

Frame and package the event in the NOW.

The secret formulas allow you to connect on numerous levels as you embark on the first steps to building a relationship. The beauty of the questions is they allow the other person to shine. They will remember how special you made them feel by taking an interest. The next time John has an order to be placed, a deal to be shared, or a person to invite to a get together, he will probably think of you.

It's that simple.

Example

Here is a personal example of the secret formulas at work.

I went to a favorite local restaurant—the food is great, it's close to home, and I enjoy the ambiance. On this particular night, I met a new server. Becky, the new server, introduced herself and asked what I would like to drink.

"Becky, it's so great to meet you. I come here often, but I've never seen you before. Where are you from?"

Becky shared that she's from Virginia and just moved here about three weeks ago. She stepped away to grab my beverage.

When Becky returned, she had a smile on her face. She was happy to serve my table.

As Becky served the main course, she mentioned that she had not been a server for very long. This was my opening.

"What did you do before?"

By the time I received my coffee and dessert, I felt comfortable asking Becky the final question:

"What is your passion, Becky?"

Her face lit up. She went on for a few minutes about her passion. The manager noticed her spending extra time at my table and asked if everything was okay.

"Absolutely! Becky is great! I just met her. What an amazing lady."

I may have contributed to her job security. It's easy to create this kind of positive energy with a few simple questions. When you do, don't be surprised when that energy is returned. You might even receive a free dessert at the end of the evening!

A VALUABLE COMMODITY

OOOOOOOOOOOOOOOOOOOOOOOOOOOOOOOOOOOOOO

I learned the value of relationships long ago. As I mentioned, I was terribly shy and insecure as a child. My parents were divorced, and I was reared by my very protective mother.

At the age of nine-and-a-half, my mom and I made a major move from Romania to Israel. We were completely penniless and looking forward to an easier life in our new home, but believe me; the first few years were not easy. I had to learn a new language and adapt to living in a dorm with orphans and other immigrant children. The kids made fun of me, because I had fine, conservative clothes and had been exposed to an abundance of culture. I knew how to study, but I was clueless about hard manual labor. It was a difficult transition.

I blossomed when my son was born. My passion for motherhood alleviated my shyness and I began to reach out to other young mothers. I also returned to work and opened myself up to new opportunities to support our little family.

Through all of these new connections, I discovered that asking questions was a terrific way to learn about people. I practiced putting others first, asking them what eventually became the three secret formula questions, and many wonderful relationships grew—both personal and business.

I cannot emphasize enough the value of these three simple questions. Learn them, practice them, and watch your life transform.

5 LEVELS OF RELATIONSHIPS

ooooooooooooooooooooooooooooooooooooooooo

As you practice building relationships, it is important to know that every relationship goes through five basic levels:

1. Pursue the relationship
2. Engage in the relationship
3. Establish the relationship
4. Nourish the relationship
5. End the relationship

Pursuing the relationship is self-explanatory. Use your three secret formulas to lay the foundation.

Engaging in the relationship is when you decide the connection is worth pursuing, so you put more time into it, extending the value of the relationship.

Establishing the relationship is simple. When you establish it, you give it a title, such as personal intimate, personal friendship, extended family friendship, family, school, business, etc.

Nourishing the relationship is extremely important. If you want it to grow, you must give it fuel. You water your plants; put food in your own body; feed the dog. When you nourish a relationship, you do things like call or text just to say hello; send a card on their birthday; make time to meet for lunch or dinner; ask them how they are doing; follow up on significant events in their lives; offer support when they are going through a tough time. These things nourish a relationship and keep it vital and healthy.

The final phase of relationships is delicate. All relationships end. This is not in our control. Some people enter our lives as simple messengers leading us to a new path; others are with us for longer periods of time. There are some relationships that are a brief encounter.

All relationships are valuable.

In business when we know a contract is coming to its final stages, we begin to pursue new opportunities outside the circle of the relationship in order to sustain our business. That is the natural cycle of business engagements.

In the personal arena, when we are in an intimate relationship, we are not to pursue another intimate relationship until we have ended the relationship we are currently in. That is taboo.

There are many ways a relationship may end—a major difference of opinion that is too difficult to overcome; growing up and growing apart emotionally; a geographical change; even death.

Nevertheless, relationships shape our lives and provide us feedback on how we are living our lives.

A friend of mine used to say, "I have reached tremendous success in my life. I feel like I am an island, powerful and independent."

I would smile and respond, "Did you get there on your own? Would you like to get off your island sometimes and see other places? Who do you expect to visit you on this island?"

He would laugh, "Okay, you made your point."

We are not islands. We don't want to be. It is human nature to move through the stages of relationships many times throughout our lives.

Now that we know the ground rules, let's look at some tips and formulas to help us with relationships in three central areas: Business, personal, and family.

BUSINESS

ooooooooooooo

New job

This is your moment to shine!

Learn—Connect—Contribute

Taboo: Don't force your plans and ideas in a new workplace too soon. Do your homework first, and then learn where you can best contribute.

Remember, you were chosen for this position by management. Now, you must display your knowledge, your people skills, and your expertise. Make them glad they hired you!

This includes opening yourself to learning from your new colleagues. The most important thing you can do, especially in your first few months, is to connect with your fellow workers. Use the three secret formula questions to get to know them. Eat lunch in the cafeteria so you have further opportunities for connections.

The first 90 days of your employment are crucial. The relationships you build during that time will directly impact your job security.

New career
A new career will shift your life from where it is to where it could be.

Dream—Listen—Change

Taboo: Don't look back on your life and wonder what could have been.

I would like to share with you a lovely story. A young gentleman was lying in a hospital bed recuperating from an injury. He was twenty-one years old at the time and facing some challenges. As he was convalescing he had conversation that changed the course of his life.

He received incredibly sage advice from the gentleman lying in the bed next to him. The man said, "It's too late for me to make changes. Don't do what I did—nothing. Now, all I can think of is what I could have been or what I should have done but didn't do."

Right then, the young man decided to change his life. He made a commitment to leave his existing career and follow his dream of becoming a personal trainer.

The young man loved his new job; but after he had been working in the field for a few years, he realized that many of his clients had eating disorders.

He decided he could do something about that problem and started a new venture that offered fresh food that was gluten free, hormone free, and organic. He prepared meals daily for clients that had just the right portions and were of the best quality. His endeavor was a huge success!

His new career shifted him from where he was to where he could be. You can do this, too! It is never too late.

Meeting a vendor for lunch

Use the three secret formulas to build a relationship with your vendor.

Always—Follow—Up

Taboo: Don't allow yourself to be distracted by cell phone calls, texts, or emails. Give your full attention to the vendor.

Meeting a vendor for lunch is a golden opportunity for relationship building.

Start with those three secret formula questions to get the ball rolling. Then actively listen. Take time to eat, and let your vendor talk.

What does your vendor need? What are his/her concerns? Be open to learning about his/her company's culture to establish a mutually beneficial connection.

Suggest a local place where you can easily communicate, or pick up a sandwich and go to a local park. Sitting outside will give both of you a sense of liberty, while also recharging your energy levels.

Called for a job interview

When a potential employer chooses to meet you in person, it's already a good sign. Feel good about yourself, and go for it!

Calm—Confident—Centered

Taboo: Don't brag! Be yourself. Show your passion quietly and skillfully.

Always dress in business attire. The importance of first impressions cannot be overstated. If you are a woman make sure your hair is neatly styled, that you are wearing light makeup, and minimal jewelry. If you are a man, neatness and cleanliness rules also apply. Make certain you present a polished and professional appearance.

All of us are nervous when we go to a job interview. Remember to breathe! There are two entities at the table, feel confident about what you have to offer.

Don't overdo it with energy or exuberance. Be yourself and let your passions shine through.

Management and relationships

A great manager learns everything about their organization from the ground up.

Follow—Flow—Free

Taboo: Don't underestimate the power of personal connections with workers, customers, and vendors.

The top requirement of a good manager is excellent people skills. Communicate with everyone you come into contact with during the course of your business day.

You will be successful if you foster a culture where employees, customers, and vendors feel comfortable approaching you to discuss and share concerns.

Follow the flow of your workplace and be a hands-on manager. Make sure everyone who works for you understands that they are free to communicate ideas, problems, or solutions.

First impressions

First impressions are of paramount importance. Take care to present yourself well.

Be Courteous—Be Focused—Be

Taboo: Don't be lazy about your appearance. Dress according to the occasion and always look clean and neat.

If you make a bad first impression you will have difficulty reversing that view. Always put your best self forward when you meet someone for the first time.

The best way to do this is by not being someone you're not. Be yourself! Focus on the other person. People will enjoy being around you if you are interested in them and put them at ease in conversation.

Flight delays

This is usually an annoyance, but you can turn it into an opportunity.

Breathe—Smile—Connect

Taboo: Don't allow your irritation negatively affect everyone around you. If you are powerless over the situation, shift your attitude and make the best of it.

I have a fun story to share related to this tip:

My girlfriend and I were scheduled to leave JFK in New York, heading home to LAX in California, but our flight was delayed due to bad weather conditions.

We waited at the terminal, and people started to get anxious and impatient. My friend and I were traveling for a vacation, however many of the travelers were in New York on business. They just wanted to get home to their families. Other passengers had connecting flights in Los Angeles and were worried they would miss them.

After about an hour, the flight attendant advised us that we might be there a long time and suggested that anyone who was able could book another flight the next day.

A few people chose that option, but most of us stayed and waited. As the tension mounted, I came up with an idea. I suggested to my girlfriend that we should turn the wait time into a fun event that would relieve the tension and anxiety of the other passengers.

I took out my business cards and approached the passengers, giving each of them my card and asking if they would like to give me theirs. "Let's see if we can network," I said, "or at least introduce ourselves and get to know each other a little better while we're waiting."

Slowly, I worked in the three secret formula questions to get the conversation going. Where are you from? What type of work do you do? What is your passion?

Everyone became interested, and within a short period of time, people were approaching me. The audience continued to grow.

Eventually, the flight attendant came over and asked what was going on.

"She's creating relationships and making the time pass more quickly!" one of the passengers replied. "We're having fun!"

We all boarded the flight forty minutes later, and everyone seemed to have benefited from our networking party.

The flight attendant rewarded me with two first-class seats.

An adverse situation became a delightful day, and some of us continued to develop our relationships after the flight.

PERSONAL

oooooooooooooo

Meeting your significant other's parents for the first time

The most important things to remember are listen and be you.

Pleasant—Polite—Profound

Taboo: Don't brag or talk too much about yourself—especially about your achievements or previous relationships.

Your significant other already loves you, so chances are his or her parents will, too. Don't try too hard. Just be yourself and enjoy getting to know the family. You may be spending quite a bit of time with them in the future!

Going out to dinner with new friends introduced by old friends

Listen more, talk less.

Follow—Free—Funny

Taboo: Do not reveal secrets about your mutual friends.

It is always awkward beginning a relationship with someone when you share a mutual friendship. You may wonder what they already know about me.

Relax, and follow your own path in getting to know each other. Free yourself from the restrictions of the other friendship and start the conversation fresh, as if you know nothing about these new potential friends. Have fun, and enjoy getting to know them.

Entertaining

It's a great way to connect with people and share the sanctuary of your home.

Invite—Mix—Enjoy

Taboo: Don't overdo it with food. More is not better; it's simply more.

Figure out in advance how many people you want to invite. Then, consider the theme of the event. Does it have a specific purpose or celebration, or is it just for the fun?

Concentrate on attractive, disposable dishes. Your main energy should go into the quality of the food, not necessarily the quantity. Order a variety of desserts from a local bakery, small bites and inviting pieces.

Make sure you let your guests know that it is casual, semi-casual, or a cocktail party. This will guarantee everyone's comfort.

Entertaining does not need to be over the top. The point is establishing connections and nourishing relationships in a comfortable and congenial atmosphere.

Here is an example of an easy event preparation:

Grill chicken in your oven or barbeque prior to your guest's arrival.

Prepare a fresh and easy homemade dressing: Avocado and dill mix with olive oil and fresh lemon juice, or poppy seed dressing to compliment mixed greens or with the dish described in the next paragraph. You could also mix various fruit juices with olive oil and a few spoons of honey and mustard.

Combine mixed grilled vegetables to simple boiled pasta. Mix in butter, finely chopped lettuce, sliced cucumbers, bell peppers, radishes, and sliced tomatoes.

Offer wine, beer, water, and sparkling water, and you're done!

Special events

Make a special event like a graduation, homecoming, or housewarming even more memorable.

Simple—Budget—Considerate

Taboo: Do not forget the person you are honoring as you plan the event.

You can go anywhere to celebrate a special event—from your own backyard to a private room at a cozy Italian restaurant. It is important to work with the person(s) you are honoring in your special event to make sure you are creating a celebration where they feel joyful and content.

Honeymoon plans

Honeymoon is comprised of two words: honey and moon.

U put the other person first and then the self (S)

Taboo: Don't plan too many activities. Take time to be still and connect with your loved one.

Honey—time with your loved one must be sweet and full of love. Moon—feel your spirit lift as high as the moon, let the light of the moon shine on you from above. The moon is magnetic. Enjoy soaking in the beauty of the moon and stars.

Your honeymoon is the ideal opportunity to nurture the relationship with the person you love and care about the most. This is the time when you build the foundation for your union.

Wedding plans—more fun, less money

Build relationships around your wedding plans. Every step should be easy and fun without landing you in the poor house!

Priorities—Passion—Financial

Taboo: Don't allow yourself to get overwhelmed in planning and forget the reason for the event—love.

Weddings have the potential to be huge opportunities for stress. Don't let that happen! Prepare a list according to your priorities, passion, and financial abilities.

Plan ahead and know it is not about the extravaganza. It's about the moment of connecting the two of you, your families, and your loved ones under the umbrella of one meaningful relationship and announcing your love to the world.

If your budget allows, hire a wedding planner to take care of the details. Make sure to shop around for one you will be able to count on.

Listen to the advice of your friends and family. If you objectively take in their suggestions, they might have some valuable advice. Ultimately it is your event. You have the final say.

Plan your event with joy and openness. Then, when you look at your wedding photos, you will see the sparkle in your eyes as you happily gaze into your future. You will share the memories of this moment with your children and generations to come. Relish the gift it brings, rather than becoming overwhelmed in the planning.

Intimate friendships

Build intimate friendships with special people in your life.

Support—Filter—Marinate

Taboo: Don't judge. Remember, it's okay to have different views. Validate each person's feelings and viewpoints.

The term intimate friendship may be confusing. Intimacy does not always mean a physical or sexual connection. It is a relationship that is built on a deeper level of trust.

Intimate friendships are wonderful, because they allow you the freedom to be vulnerable. You trust your intimate friends to tell you the truth and not to use the information you share with them in negatively. Intimate friendships are effective in lowering stress and allowing us to feel more content and happy.

I love to cultivate intimate friendships. I have a small family, so my intimate friends are precious to me. They walk with me along the path of life, and I am lucky and blessed by our connections.

Sometimes your ultimate intimate friend is your mate, and in this case, your connection creates a full circle of mind, body, and spirit. This is a true gift.

The most important thing to remember in nurturing intimate friendships is that you will not agree on everything. Honor your different views—validate your feelings and the feelings of your friend. Rather than responding quickly in a disagreement, take time out. Lengthen your fuse, and listen.

If you take a time before responding, you are able to filter or marinate your response. How you react can deposit tremendous beauty into the relationship, especially when it's a full-circle connection.

Stay focused in the chaos

When you are in the middle of a huge life event, find ways to center yourself in the middle of the storm.

Share—Hear—Experience

Taboo: Don't hide from the storm. None of us are guaranteed smooth sailing.

None of us get to skate through life without experiencing some chaos. When you are faced with a troubling event, the best thing is to stay still for a moment. Let the event sink in.

Then, reach out to your closest friends, family members, or coworkers for support. You have spent a lot of time cultivating healthy relationships. Now is the time to lean on them for guidance.

Share the details of the event and become an audience member rather than the lead player. Listen for prudent advice. The different perspectives offered by your support system may hold a solution that will guide you out of the chaos.

Time off—recharging your batteries

This is the time to connect with the present and refuel your energy level.

Rest—Review—Refuel

Taboo: Don't permit work to seep into your time off. The best way to recharge your batteries is to completely unplug from your job and regular responsibilities.

Time off is critical to your health and wellbeing. It is also good for relationships, as you are more receptive after you have had time to recharge your own batteries.

Take time to meditate, exercise, observe your surroundings and be still. Go for a long walk. Meet a close friend for coffee, lunch, or a drink.

Alone time

Alone time is a special time when you are free to tap into your feelings and negotiate with your nature.

Reflect—Dream—Link

Taboo: Don't share this time with anyone else. It is essential to spend some time completely alone to listen to your heart.

This is an absolute must. You need to develop your relationship with yourself, too. What are your dreams? How do you feel?

Do you wish you could exercise more or eat healthier? Check in with your physical wellbeing. Believe it or not, a healthy relationship with food automatically shifts your relationship with exercise and even money.

How about your emotional health? Are you surrounding yourself with positive, healthy relationships, or do you attract the crazies who sabotage your success? Are you leading the life you want, or do you see a different path ahead? Give yourself permission during this alone time to dream.

Spend at least one hour a week with yourself. You may find you're excellent company!

Intimacy and the crumbs in between

Crumbs or friction will eventually appear in any intimate relationship. How you brush them away is the key. The sweets must exceed the crumbs!

Facts—Filter—Freedom

When we realistically observe facts and filter our words and actions, we will be free of the stress induced by friction in a relationship.

Taboo: Don't expect your partner to be the sole provider of your happiness, contentment, or confidence.

One of my favorite areas of relationships—one that entirely warms our hearts, lifts our moods, colors our spirits, and tickles our bodies is the beginning.

The relationship starts when two strangers meet. For whatever reason, this person enters your space, and your life is changed forever.

You may also meet someone via the Internet or social media. Nevertheless, you are connected. Now what?

For some of us, we instantly know if there is a connection, a sense of chemistry, a desire to know more about each other and spend as much time together as possible.

I would like to share some of my tips that may be valuable from the moment you make that first connection.

Let's say you meet at a party and instantly feel that special connection. Keep talking! Spend time together; even walk outside for more intimate conversation. But remember, you were invited to this party by friends or family members. Be polite and courteous to your host and fellow guests. Don't completely disappear! If the connection is truly there, you will have time to learn more about each other later. If you both feel the spark, exchange information and plan another time to get together.

Perhaps you meet at the supermarket, the local dry cleaner's, or a gas station. Go ahead and exchange numbers if you think there is real potential. Then, go about your day. Don't disrupt your plans. One of you will call the other within a day or two if you are really interested.

When you speak on the phone or via email, find out more about each other before your first official date. It will give you more to talk about when you see each other again.

By the way, the first date should be no longer than two hours. Keep it simple; let it flow easily. If this is meant to be, it will be healthier if you allow it to grow naturally.

Let's get to the core of the relationship— the intimacy and the crumbs in between.

What do I mean by the crumbs in between? Have you ever eaten a meal in bed or a snack on the couch, and later you felt annoyed by the crumbs you left behind? It's irritating, isn't it?

These crumbs represent friction, and in relationships that friction comes in the moments we don't feel love. We desire our previous freedom and independence. We resent the commitment we made and the compromises that are part of that journey.

Believe me, the crumbs will show up throughout your relationship. I know this from personal experience. I had several marriages and relationships end because of the crumbs. Looking back, I know each of those events was a great learning experience. They were awakenings for me at those times in my life when I was still learning about relationships and intimacy. It was important to not walk away angry or upset, but to move forward and out of the relationship with new wisdom.

My relationships represent individual chapters in my life, and I cherish them deeply and guard them with respect. I appreciate the education they offer me—both my sweets and my crumbs.

The secret is to watch for the crumbs and try to avoid them. . It is also important to recognize that there will be days when the crumbs are more irritating than other days. That's okay. We're human. We can learn to get through those times.

So let's shift from the crumbs to the sweets—those special moments when we feel on top of the world. Nothing bothers us. We are proactive when we face challenges feeling no fear or anxiety.

When we're in this space in a relationship, we see nothing negative. Our partner is perfect. We are perfect together. Everything is absolutely as it should be, and life is good

We can hardly wait to get together again, and our day seems endless before we rush back into each other's arms.

This kind of personal intimacy takes over ninety-five percent of your relationship. This is true whether you are a teenager, a young adult, middle age, or older. You are in love with love, and you feel incredibly grateful and fortunate to have found that special someone.

Then, reality sinks in. I don't want to sound pessimistic, but a brilliant person told me that we would be better at gauging relationships if we did our homework and tested them like we do our hairdresser or dentist. If you get a bad haircut, do you go back to the same person?

But this is not the case with personal intimate relationships. We become emotionally involved and common sense goes out the window. We may even start to believe that person is the source of our happiness or confidence. That is a dangerous place to be.

Somewhere in the first giddy days of romance, we often forget that we are two separate people. We have different passions, views, hobbies, outlooks, and visions. Eventually, we're going to disagree. How we handle those differences is the key to the success of our relationship.

Here are some practical tips I have collected over the years. These tips helped me navigate the sweets and the crumbs of intimate relationships:

1. Validate your partner's feelings.
2. Learn about your partner's past.
3. Don't be a narcissist.
4. Take care of yourself.
5. Respect your partner.
6. Ask the important question: What is your passion? Do this at least once a year

7. Spend at least one to two hours of quality time each week with your partner outside of the home. Use this time to share everything that is on your mind and in your heart.

8. Do at least one or two activities every week that keep your identities alive.

9. Always make time for hugs and kisses.

10. Don't ask a million questions right when your partner walks in the door.

11. Do spontaneous things—give flowers, a card, or dress up just because you feel like it.

12. Take at least three days a year to go somewhere together outside of your zip code, to build your intimacy and remove yourselves from outside distractions.

13. Have sexual intercourse at least twice a week, unless one of you is sick or physically unable.

14. Communicate your frustrations when the timing is right, and shift that personal intimacy from ninety-five percent to five percent of the relationship.

15. Take pride in your appearance, even when you are home doing chores.

16. Make homemade meals and treats your partner loves.

17. Respect your partner's extended family.

18. Don't argue about finances. Discuss them together and use common sense when deciding what portion of your income goes to household expenses and what will be used for fun.

19. Let your partner be your best friend.

20. Discuss your plans around social events and family events.

21. Take walks together.

22. Listen to music.

23. Don't criticize. Offer support and kind ideas.

24. Listen to your tone of voice when you express yourself. Allow your thoughts to marinate and filter before you speak out loud.
25. Never go to bed angry.
26. Make time for pillow talk. It's a great way to close the day!

It took me many years to understand the value of a close intimate relationship. It is lovely to listen to the falling rain together, watch a movie, listen to music, or just lie in bed and hold each other. No words need to be exchanged. This is what I call a great connection, a relationship that will separate the crumbs from the sweets.

We will have days when we agree to disagree, when we are both tired from a long and stressful day. Regardless of outside stress, don't go to bed angry. Eat dinner together, go for a walk or exercise, or do the next thing on your list, and by the time you slip comfortably between the sheets, the crumbs are gone.

The work of a great relationship is learning to connect and reconnect with the chemistry and passion that initially brought you together. I hope the tips I have provided will be tools to help you accomplish that.

Our relationships grow when we grow up and learn to plant that sweet seed together and nourish it along the way.

In the event you find too many crumbs in your relationship, and they are too big and irritating to sweep away, it may be time to consider a change.

There is someone for everyone, and intimate relationships are not one size fits all. Take your time to find your perfect fit.

Follow the relationship steps I mentioned earlier, and if you see your relationship coming to an end, don't spend too much time, energy, or money on its dissolution. Release the anger or disappointment, and give yourself a chance to move on and take what you have learned into a new situation.

One more delightful tip:

Start your day with a smile, a hug, and a kiss. Never forget to say I love you; have a happy day. You will feel great, your partner will feel great, and so will your children.

FAMILY

ooooooooo

Travel with friends/family members

Traveling with friends or family can be delightful.

Respect—Discuss—Fun

Taboo: Do not force your itinerary on the group.

You must start with a respectful relationship prior to making travel plans. Discuss ideas, dates, and locations, as well as budgets, hobbies, and passions. Make sure everyone traveling with the group has an opportunity to share their thoughts and vote on the final itinerary.

Once you arrive at your destination, concentrate on one thing: FUN!

You will not always agree on each day's itinerary. Within the trip give each other opportunities for private time. The key is to spend some quality time together.

Relocation

It's time to move! Make it an adventure instead of a headache.

Research—Explore—Join

Taboo: Don't isolate when you arrive in your new community. Get out of the house and meet your neighbors, local merchants, and new co-workers.

What do you do first? Do your homework! When scouting for locations to rent or own, research the local housing market. How far will your home be from your job? Can you utilize public transportation? If you have children, learn about the school systems. Check out the area—walk and drive around and take note of what you like and what you don't like.

When you move in, immediately start making connections. Introduce yourself to the neighbors. Connect with the local dry cleaner, hairdresser, or barber shop owner. Dine at neighborhood restaurants. Go in to pay at the gas station and say hello, rather than paying at the pump and speeding off.

Relocation can be an exhilarating experience. There is so much to learn about a new location. Have fun exploring! Visit local places of worship or discover what community groups might be of interest to you. Buy tickets to a concert, or wander through a museum. Soon you will be building relationships all over town.

Purchase a house

Choose a home that is a safe haven; an inviting place where you, your family, and friends feel comfortable.

Safe—Comfortable—Happy

Taboo: Do not fill your home with clutter. Learn what items are unnecessary and remove them.

This is a great moment. Purchasing a new home is a huge decision. Let the realtor know exactly what you desire, where you would like to locate, and a financial range within your comfort zone.

When you move in, decorate your home with cheerful colors. The mood of your home will have an impact on you every day.

Visit your local home furniture store or outlets where they sell unused model home furniture. You may find a terrific deal on something new to give your home just the right touch.

Build relationships with local art shops and appliance outlets and gradually equip your home with useful items that increase your delight.

Your relationship with your home is a lasting one and it requires continual care.

Purchase a car

The most important action is to establish proper contacts.

Build—Negotiate—Enjoy

Taboo: Do not follow your first impulse. Do your homework and educate yourself about this transaction.

Start your education on the Internet to avoid chasing all over town for the best deal. Develop a list of your criteria for the perfect car, and then make phone calls to convey your request clearly and directly. Now, you are ready to go to the car lot.

Take time to negotiate and build a relationship with car dealers. You will enjoy your new car more when you know you made an informed decision.

Moving into a new home

Moving does not have to be a problematic event. Make the most of this event to get rid of things you don't need, clean house, and buy new items to decorate your new home.

Toss—Hire—Buy

Taboo: Don't try to do it alone. Get help.

Most people hate to move. I validate their feelings, but moving into a new home is a terrific opportunity. It is a chance for spring cleaning, downsizing, and reevaluating what is important to you in a home.

I strongly urge you to search for a reputable company and hire them to pack the heavy stuff and unpack and set up your new place. If you can afford it, this makes the transition smoother.

If you enlist friends and family to make the move, make sure to thank them with a pizza party at the end of the day or a coupon to their favorite movie theater or restaurant. Their time is valuable. Don't take it for granted as free labor.

House maintenance and repairs

You introduced yourself to your home. Now your home is introducing itself to you—the good, the bad, and the ugly.

Check—Care—Nourish

Taboo: Don't panic. When you discover something in your home that needs fixing, take immediate action.

Homes, like cars and people require nourishment and care. Walk around your home and get an overview of its health once a week, and once a month give it a serious check-up.

Pay attention to cracks in walls, water leaks, furniture that is in need of repair and other changes you discover.

If you don't know how to fix the item yourself, find an expert. Build relationships with local painters, electricians, plumbers, and other handymen (and women) in your area.

When someone comes to work on your home, make sure to offer them water. If the job requires longer hours, offer fruit, nuts, or make them a sandwich or burrito. They may decline, but it's important to nourish this business relationship with common courtesies.

At the end of the job, tip the worker. You are investing in future good service. If the bill is $80, offer a $5 or $6 tip; if it's over $100, offer at least $10.

The power of home cooking

Home cooking is wonderful! It nourishes your family and creates healthy habits for years to come.

Portion—Preparation—Love

Taboo: Don't skip this very important family activity. It nurtures your family emotionally as well as physically.

Why is home cooking so important? Because you put a bit of yourself into it; YOU create the healthy meal, considering portion and preparation. Use good, fresh ingredients, seasoned with a dash of love.

It's rewarding to sit down together as a family, eat a delicious meal, and share the experiences of the day. When you create a homemade meal, you strengthen the relationships with the people living with you under the same roof. Also, the leftovers make a great lunch the next day!

When you regularly cook at home, you are more aware of your pantry inventory, the food in your freezer, and other products available to compile a nice meal.

On occasion make the meal an impromptu event and involve the entire family. This allows additional time for nourishing relationships and offers hands-on training for healthy eating habits.

Meeting an old relative or extended family member for the first time

This is a huge moment. Embrace the power of family.

Embrace—Build—Honor

Taboo: Don't allow differing views create conflict. It's not worth it.

Drop assumptions based on what you have heard about the person from other friends or relatives. Develop your own relationship by asking questions and being a great listener.

Remember, the person may be uncomfortable during this first-time meeting. Do your part to create a fun, relaxed, and easy gathering. Avoid talking about money, religion, or politics, and a harmonious occasion will be enjoyed by all.

IGI PRINCIPLES AND ETM FORMULAS

ooooooooooooooooooooooooooo

Are you beginning to grasp the idea that the power of success is in the connections? But how do we strengthen these connections? How do we successfully link our energy and emotions with the concrete side of our minds; the logical, practical thinker in each of us to make the best of every situation?

This is exactly what I would like to share with you. I have developed simple solutions to strengthen connections between your emotional side and your practical side to boost your trajectory toward success. These solutions come in two steps:

Step 1: IGI Principles
Step 2: ETM Formulas

Let's break down each step.

IGI Principles

IGI stands for **Intentions Grounded** in **Intuition**. Practicing this principle will give you a foundation for successful relationships.

Intentions determine the outcome of your life. They set the path. To me, intention is the difference between wandering around in the wilderness and having a roadmap that points you in the right direction. Your intention is a powerful tool on the road to success. It influences every decision you make.

Grounded is where your practical nature comes in. Throughout life's journey it is important to use common sense. Successful people are not only dreamers; they are also doers. We may have a desire to fly, but part of us needs to be there to hold the kite string that keeps us anchored to the ground. We have to practice utilizing our logical minds as well as our hearts to succeed.

Intuition is something we all possess, but is often overlooked as insignificant. Intuition is closely linked to success in the circle of life. When we acknowledge our intentions and apply our common sense, we become more intuitive. We start to feel at a gut level what is good for us and what is not.

Intentions Grounded in Intuition is one IGI Principle. To add to your success toolbox, let me introduce you to a few more IGI Principles.

INTRODUCING—GROWING—IMMEDIATE

Introducing. Everything in life begins with an introduction. It's that exciting moment in when you can almost taste the potential. Anything is possible. For that reason, introductions are extremely important. Remember, you never get a second chance to make a first impression. Bring your best self to every introduction.

Growing. We grow through every moment and every connection we make with another human being. The goal in life is to never stop growing, changing, improving and learning. Seize every opportunity to grow in your business and personal life.

Immediate. We live in a society of instant gratification. Technology has brought almost everything to our fingertips. But in the process, we have lost our patience. We hate to wait for anything, especially success. The word immediate is a reminder to enjoy the process. Take in the 360° view. Your immediate satisfaction is in enjoying the present.

INSPIRATION—GENEROSITY—INTELLIGENCE

Inspiration. What inspires you? Tack the word inspiration on your refrigerator and take a few minutes three times a week to think about where you derive inspiration in your life. Then, follow that inspiration.

Generosity. Living an abundant life starts with you. Be generous with your time, your money, and your energy. You will be surprised how your life will shift. When you are generous, you will receive generosity in return.

Intelligence. Apply your intelligence and common sense to every situation. Check your words before you speak. Consider your actions before you act. Give yourself time between the idea and the execution of the idea to make sure you are making the right move. If you filter your words and actions through your intelligence and common sense, you will spend less time on damage control and more time traveling toward success.

INTEREST—GOING—IDEAS

Interest. What interests you? We have countless options for learning in today's technologically savvy world. Pay attention to what grabs your attention and pursue that interest. You are more apt to be successful in an endeavor that holds your interest.

Going. Get going! Travel outside of your zip code. There is a whole new world outside of your home, and it is worth exploring. If you are willing to learn about other places and cultures, your life will be truly enriched. Don't be afraid of exploring the world. There is much to gain out there.

Ideas. Every successful endeavor starts with an idea. Allow your ideas to flow freely, then step back and consider the intentions behind each of those thoughts. Some ideas will bear fruit and others will not. You may already intuitively know which ones have a greater chance of success. Go with your gut, and pursue those ideas first.

The ETM Formulas are the second set of keys that will open the door to the race car that will speed you along the Circle of Success. They are real-world applications for your day-to-day life, and are powerful paths to activating the IGI Principles.

ETM Formulas

Of course, the first ETM Formula includes three ingredients we cannot live without: **Energy**, **Time**, and **Money**!

This is the root of your success.

Now, let me introduce additional ETM Formulas that I have designed for you.

EAT—TAKE—MAKE

Eat. This one is simple. Eat nutritional foods that provide you energy and vitality. When we fill ourselves with empty calories, that's exactly what we get, nothing! Eat foods that fuel you and speed you on the road to success.

Take. Take care of yourself. This seems like a no-brainer, but we tend to put ourselves last when life becomes hectic. No matter how crazy life gets, take time to enjoy a new hobby, go to a movie, or take a walk. Personal time is essential for your happiness and success. Take the time to nourish your body, mind, and spirit; and you will find you are better prepared to thrive in your personal and professional life.

Make. Make time for your friends and loved ones. Time moves swiftly. You don't want to discover too late that you didn't spend enough time with the people you love. Give them the attention they deserve today.

EXERCISE—TRUST—MEET

Exercise. The key is to find a type of exercise you enjoy; whether it's walking, playing basketball, riding a bike, running, yoga, or another activity. Experiment with the possibilities, then choose an exercise option that brings you joy. Carve out two to three hours a week to engage in exercise. You don't have to pick just one! Switch it up, if you like variety. You will notice a difference in your energy level and your attitude.

Trust. Trust yourself. We all have inner nudges that offer clues about how we are feeling and where we want to go in life. Trust those inner thoughts, and trust your energy level. If your energy level is consistently low when you engage in a particular activity, that action may not be the best choice. Trust yourself. Deep down, you know what's right for you.

Meet. Meetings are important. They foster stronger connections with the people around you and an enhanced sense of understanding. Schedule short meetings at work, and discuss areas of opportunity. Connect to uncover solutions and also cross-train your employees, so all business aspects are addressed; even if someone has to attend to a personal matter or is out sick. Meet with your family members around the dinner table. Turn off cell phones and other distractions, and pay attention to each other. Share your plans for the week and ask questions about how everyone is feeling and what they are hoping to accomplish during the coming days.

The same is true for friends. Find a mutually convenient time, even if it's just a half hour for a quick cup of coffee and find out how they are doing. Many of us suffer in silence when things are not going well, but a simple question from a friend can provide someone the courage to ask for help.

ENTERTAIN—TRY—MOTIVATE

Entertain. Entertainment is essential to self-replenishment. It is not only recreation, but it gives us a place for re-creation, and re-molding ourselves into better people. Entertain others in your home. Make your home a welcoming place to get together, unwind, enjoy each other's company, and learn and grow together.

Try. Try new things: foods you have never eaten before; a new bold color to wear to work; a new exercise routine; a new pair of shoes; a fun hairstyle; a new hair color; even a new configuration of your living room furniture. Change is good. It snaps you out of boring routines and allows you to view life from different angles.

Motivate. Motivate yourself with music. Music has a unique way of affecting your soul. It has the power to entertain, calm, energize, or soothe you simply through listening. Try adding music to a task you do not particularly enjoy, like cleaning the kitchen, doing laundry, or any number of household chores. You will find motivation through music.

Now that you have these principles and formulas as guides, go for it! Use them to strengthen your relationships. Focus on these actions, and your life will move in the direction of success. These principles worked for me, and I am certain they will work for you.

LOG IT

ooooooooo

O n the next few pages, you will find sample charts to help you track your relationships. I encourage you to use these as guides to focus on nourishing your personal, business, and family relationships. You may want to save these logs electronically as a relationship database. You never know when an old friend may become a new business partner!

New Relationships (business)
Name:
Contact:
Nature:
Comments:
Name:
Contact:
Nature:
Comments:

Name:
Contact:
Nature:
Comments:
Name:
Contact:
Nature:
Comments:
New Relationships (social)
Name:
Contact:
Comments:
Name:
Contact:
Comments:
Name:
Contact:
Comments:
Name:
Contact:
Comments:
Name:
Contact:
Comments:

Intimate Relationships
Name:
Contact:
Comments:
Name:
Contact:
Comments:
Name:
Contact:
Comments:
Name:
Contact:
Comments:
Name:
Contact:
Comments:
Intimate Relationships (personal)
Name:
Contact:
Comments:
Name:
Contact:
Comments:

Name:
Contact:
Comments:
Name:
Contact:
Comments:
Name:
Contact:
Comments:
Work Relationships
Name:
Department:
Job Title:
Comments:
Name:
Department:
Job Title:
Comments:
Name:
Department:
Job Title:
Comments:
Name:
Department:
Job Title:
Comments:

I hope this section presented you with useful actions to take in the area of relationships. Don't get stuck on an island. Nourish your connections, and you will taste the fruits of a successful life.

PART III

ENERGY—SPARK IT, DON'T SAP IT

We'll now transition to the third important element for 360° success: Energy. In this section, we will learn to shift our mindsets and perform tasks that energize rather than sap our energy. We will also discover how crucial it is to develop positive energy. Energy is not only fuel for getting things done; it is also the magnetic force that draws people to you.

It is my mission to supply tools to help reignite your passion. When you light that spark, you will feel your energy soars. Let's start with a few warm-up questions:

What impacts your energy level?
Why is energy so important?
What do you do with energy?

Have you considered these questions before? Energy is critical to success. It is also an elusive concept. We struggle to maintain positive energy flow, especially when things do not go according to plan. We want this, we want that, we want it all! Why shouldn't we have it all? We deserve it! But when we get down to the hard work of achieving goals, it's difficult to gather the energy we need to get the job done.

I learned that I can set the process in motion and plug into an abundant energy source by simply shifting my outlook on life. If my attitude is positive, I am filled with more than enough energy to overcome day-to-day challenges. However, if my attitude is negative, I can barely drag myself through the day.

Have you experienced this? Reflect upon how your outlook on life impacts your energy level. You may be surprised to see how closely they are linked.

Energy is also impacted by your emotional state of mind. Do you feel like your emotions are always running in high gear? Emotions will quickly drain your energy source. Depression is another serious enemy of your energy levels. Turbulent feelings can deplete your energy in a matter of minutes.

Do you feel you have been violated by a particular event, person, or situation? Do you find yourself making numerous emotional decisions in your business or personal life? Do you tend to make snap decisions just to get through a situation, so that you can just move on? Emotions are directly linked to energy levels. In this section we will further explore the link between energy and emotion.

Now that I have you thinking, let's explore all the different ways we can draw great, positive energy into our 360° sphere. We will begin with the food we eat.

EAT THE FOODS
THAT LOVE YOU BACK

ooooooooooooooooooooooooooooo

I spent years battling with food and looking for love. To be honest, I wasn't very successful on either front. Finally, I started to realize I was missing some key elements. It hit me right between the eyes that I would never find peace of mind, personal freedom, or love by building an unhealthy relationship with food. These things were connected.

I went on a quest to change my relationship with food. My expedition led me to develop a powerful, effective, and user-friendly program that has worked for hundreds of my coaching clients as well.

This program will change your life!

How so?

The program will change you in three significant ways:

1. It will show you how to link your emotions with common sense, so you are able to make logical choices that establish a healthy relationship with food, instead of emotional decisions that create an unhealthy relationship with food.
2. It will build an amazing friendship with food. Food will become your ally—that all-important ingredient that not only sustains your life but increases your happiness every time you make nourishing choices.
3. It will color your daily life with sizzling energy, a sunny attitude, and a brilliant focus on whatever fate throws your way.

The problem with many diets is they are hard to maintain when life becomes chaotic. Let's face it; life gets hectic all the time! When was the last time you had a day that went completely according to plan? Cars get flat tires, kids get sick, hurricanes blow through town, and life is anything but predictable.

In the first section we discussed developing a relationship with money. The same is true for food. Neither of these elements are your enemy. They both can be your friend and partner in achieving a successful and fulfilling life.

This program will help you to maintain a healthy relationship with food. You will discover the exact foods that love you back. What better motivation for healthy nutrition than to recognize the foods that make you feel great?

Let's get started!

BUILDING A RELATIONSHIP

ooooooooooooooooooooooooooooooooooooooooo

Do you have a healthy relationship with food?
Is food the enemy—a foe you do battle with daily?

Food should be fun.
—Thomas Keller

I would like you to ask yourself three questions about how you feel today:

My energy today is:

Excellent	Good	So-So	Weak	Blah
1	2	3	4	5

My mood today is:

Excellent	Good	So-So	Weak	Blah
1	2	3	4	5

My focus today is:

Excellent	Good	So-So	Weak	Blah
1	2	3	4	5

Your energy, mood, and focus are directly affected by what you put in your body.

According to CBS News, two-thirds of Americans are overweight or obese. That is more than 190 million people! Numbers like these raise our panic level. We have fallen so far it seems as though we will never recover. How will we reverse this trend? What is going on?

Another recent poll revealed that seven out of ten people in the United States are anxious about money. Is there a relationship between the two? Financial stress has been linked to health problems such as depression, sleep deprivation, and eating disorders.

Our relationship with food ranges from healthy to unhealthy for a variety of reasons. In this program, I will explain how to change your relationship with food. It is not a diet. It is an opportunity to build a new relationship with food that will have an incredible impact on the rest of your life.

This is a guilt-free program. Guilt is a wasted emotion. I am not the food police, telling you everything you can't eat. Instead, I will open the door for you to make your own decisions.

Most of us, especially in the United States have easy access to a tremendous variety of foods. You are free to develop your own personal and *successful* relationship with food by sampling different flavors and then logically assessing which foods are your favorites.

WHY DO I CARE?

ooooooooooooooooooooooo

I care because I used to have a terrible relationship with food. I changed that relationship, and I can't begin to describe the improvement in my life.

I want to share what I have learned.

My poor relationship with food began as a young girl. Difficult emotional periods had a direct link to my stomach. I often turned to food for consolation, but my choices made me feel worse about myself.

I was bulimic and then I became anorexic. My stomach became so small that it rejected most food; even my favorites, like ice cream, coffee, pickles, tuna, and strawberries. I would push a plate of food away from me, claiming I didn't need it. But I did. We all need nourishment to live and thrive.

My miserable relationship with food would not have changed had I not realized that love, emotions, and food are intertwined. It was important for me to learn to nurture healthier connections in all of those areas, or food would always be the enemy.

I would like to encourage you to try an experiment. The next time you go to the grocery store, observe what people place in their carts.

This is what I saw the last time I went to the store:

A very thin young woman placed vegetables in her cart and a few pieces of fruit. She also added some protein products and bottled water. There was no bread or other carbohydrates.

A heavyset woman in her late forties, toting a couple of children, placed potatoes, beans, pasta, a loaf of bread, butter, bananas, juice, cereal, and some chicken in her cart.

A woman in her thirties shopped with her husband. They looked fit and happy. I glanced in their cart and saw a bar of dark chocolate, fish, yams, apples, grapes, avocados, lettuce, various additional vegetables, ground sirloin, and eggs.

It doesn't take a degree in psychology to make a few educated guesses about the food relationships that were going on in each example.

Are you happy with the items in your grocery cart? Or do you feel that they're not offering the nourishment you need? Are you eating the foods that love you back? You'll find out as we walk through this program.

The belly rules the mind.
—Spanish Proverb

When I learned to deal with life's challenges, changes, and choices in a mature way; less emotional and more solution-oriented I realized that a healthy relationship with food is more rewarding and less painful than before.

I cultivated a new recipe for my life. It started with a big dose of common sense. Then, I siphoned off the emotional turmoil. And finally, I infused the recipe with a bit of heart. This recipe freed me to let go of my emotional weight and eat the foods that loved me back. Food and I became friends.

Many years later I realize that I was hungry for love, not food. I was starving for attention, not nourishment. That is what set up my dysfunctional relationship with food.

BREAK IT DOWN

oooooooooooooooooooooo

Let's start by breaking down our goal. You will probably agree that the most important words are:

- EAT
- FOODS
- LOVE
- BACK

I want to address each word separately.

Eat

All of us must eat to survive. The simple act of putting food in our bodies is an event that brings us nourishment and energy to live. It's essential to life.

Foods

Here is the tricky part. You choose what you eat, how you eat, how much you eat, and when you eat.

There are endless possibilities for the foods you put in your body, and we all have different preferences. I recently interviewed a sampling of people in Los Angeles and a sampling of tourists on a European cruise. I was stunned by the results. I posed one question: Tell me the three things you love to eat the most.

Here are some of the responses:

- Hamburgers, French fries, ice cream
- Chicken soup, salad, watermelon
- Danish, popcorn, chilidogs
- Broccoli, fried rice, salmon

One guy proudly said, "Steak five days a week—with a huge baked potato and baked beans."

Out of all the people I interviewed I never got the same answer twice. What are your three favorite foods?

Love

Love is the secret to this entire program. One of our basic desires is to give and receive love. But who is the person we should honor first and foremost?

Yourself!

When we love ourselves, that love grows within us, and we have more of it to share. However, when we put ourselves down and deprive ourselves of love, our bodies react by searching for love in all the wrong places; unhealthy relationships, abuse of drugs and alcohol, and overeating or eating foods that leave us empty.

Love is one of those things that diet experts seldom discuss, but love is an indispensable ingredient to a healthy relationship with food.

Back

Back represents the cyclical nature of this program. If you take positive steps, those actions will come back to you in magnificent ways. Choosing a food that tastes good, brings you energy and the right kind of nourishment encourages you to select that food again, thus creating a healthy circle of nutrition. You continue to revisit the foods that make you feel invigorated and provide what you need.

I consider my own body when I think of the word *back*. Often times, we don't want to see the whole picture. We know we don't feel good about our bodies, so we avoid taking inventory. But it's important to get in front of a couple of mirrors and examine you from all angles—front and back. Get a realistic view of where you are today, and then you will be inspired to make changes in your lifestyle that will enable you feel and look better.

Do not remain in the dark. Be brave. Look at yourself from every angle—a 360° view—and resolve to reveal your true and healthy self.

When we link the tangible product (food) and the action (eat) with the emotion (love) and create a balanced relationship between all three, we learn to manage life differently. We start a pattern of new choices that can be repeated (back). We don't damage ourselves. Instead, we love and care for ourselves as we weigh everything on a scale of logic and common sense.

BEFORE YOU BEGIN

ooooooooooooooooooooooooooo

Before you embark on this journey, I suggest you try a cleansing procedure. You may have heard of different cleansing options, but they are often used to facilitate rapid weight loss.

That is not my purpose.

I will offer you several choices of cleansing methods that have worked for me (and countless others). These methods are intended to rid your body of toxins. These cleansing events will jumpstart you on your adventure; changing toxic habits into healthy and invigorating habits.

First Choice

For an entire day, drink lukewarm water with fresh, organic lemon juice and a few teaspoons of organic honey (if you need to sweeten it).

I am not kidding about ALL day. Keep this glass by your side and continue sipping it during all your waking hours.

Second Choice

This option has nothing to do with what you eat or drink. Write the following mantra on a note card and say it to yourself over and over for one whole day before you start my program.

I am in charge of what I eat.
I will choose options that fit my lifestyle.
I will listen to my body.

Third Choice

Eat a soft-boiled egg with a dash of salt and drink a cup of white tea for breakfast.

Then, drink your next two meals. Blend one banana, one apple, one orange, one teaspoon of honey, two carrots, and two tablespoons of granola into a tasty shake.

3 STEPS—30 DAYS

oooooooooooooooooooooooo

Now that we know where we want to go with our relationship with food, how are we going to get there?

Don't worry! I have a map. We can get there in three easy steps and thirty days.

Here are the three steps to eating the foods that love you back:

Step 1: Befriend all foods. Try everything; grains, vegetables, fruits, meats, fish, honey, nuts. Variety is the spice of life, and you may discover that you actually enjoy the taste of some foods you've never tried before.

The one catch to this step is that you do not befriend packaged or canned foods (with the exception of sardines, tuna, and herring). This experiment is intended for fresh, real, non-processed food.

Step 2: Do a gut check. Tap into how you feel after each meal. You may want to keep a food journal. Write down what you ate and then assess how you feel in three main areas:

- Mood
- Energy Level
- Acuteness of Mind

This is where you truly begin to discover what foods truly love you back. When you eat carrots, do you feel extra energetic? Perhaps certain types of meat make you feel a little sluggish. Spicy homemade salsa might give you a mental kick you never noticed before.

I can't give you an answer key to this step. We are all unique, so our bodies react differently to the food we eat. The foods that are the best for me may not be the same as your top foods. Take notes and learn what foods love you back and the items you want to avoid. The results will show up loud and clear if you pay attention.

Food is an important part of a balanced diet.
—Fran Lebowitz

Step 3: Color your world. When you put together your main meals, take a look at your plate. There should be at least three different colors on your dish with equal portions of each color. Also, your portions should not exceed three-fourths the total size of an average round dinner plate.

Three equally divided portions are particularly important in this program, as they assist you in developing positive eating habits. We often tend to load up on one item that we know we really enjoy (like pasta), and then we put a tiny piece of broccoli on our plate and assume we're covered. That's cheating! Even out your portions, and you will reap the benefits of balanced, healthy eating.

Another terrific habit to acquire is to walk away from the table when you are seventy-five to eighty percent full. Don't eat until you can barely roll yourself away from your chair. If you leave the table before you are stuffed, you will accelerate your metabolism and therefore burn foods faster and more efficiently. This will also aid in digestion and make it easier to maintain a healthy body weight.

Adding a variety of color when preparing your meals creates a nutritious and visually pleasing dish. Food that is rich in color is also usually rich in nutrients. It's an easy way to make great choices for your meals.

Follow these three steps for thirty days, and you will soon have a terrific list of foods that love you back. It may not be love at first sight, but with practice and time, your relationship with food will be successful, happy, and loving. Imagine how different you will feel when you start to actively choose foods that help you thrive physically and mentally!

TRY IT, YOU'LL LIKE IT

ooooooooooooooooooooooooooooo

As I mentioned, I can't tell you specifically what foods will love you back. We are all different. But I will help you get started by offering a few sample meal choices that were successful with numerous people who experimented with this program.

As a little girl back in Romania, one of my favorite meals was toasted dark bread with cream cheese or chopped eggs. We would also mix the cream cheese with chopped radishes, bell peppers of all colors, onions, and a slice of tomato or cucumber when it was in season.

Now that I am in America, the land of abundance, I can make this sandwich anytime! I have tried many different combinations, improvising with chopped avocado, eggplant, lemon, and olive oil. I encourage you to give this tasty meal a try. You can create your own favorite sandwich, filled with all sorts of colors and delicious flavors.

Here is a list of other foods that make me feel good from the inside out:

- Grilled chicken
- Baked potato
- Pasta with vegetables
- Omelet with feta cheese
- Prime rib with broccoli and yams
- Baked tilapia with carrots and brown rice
- Baked beans with baked turkey
- Stuffed bell peppers with ground beef, brown rice, and minced onion
- Shredded white and purple cabbage with olive oil and grilled salmon
- Baked halibut with pineapple and green peas

One of my favorite ways to eat chicken or tilapia is to bake them with fresh pineapple or pear slices, lemon juice, sliced onion, and one tablespoon of honey. It's delicious!

Here is another very special dish for you to try. It is my gift to you!

Salmon Pate

- Grill the salmon
- Grill onions
- Mix the grilled salmon with the grilled onions and chop fine
- Add slivered, peeled raw almonds and bell peppers (red, yellow, orange, or green) as decoration
- Add a teaspoon of mustard

- Add 2 soft-boiled eggs; or if you are not a fan of eggs, one tablespoon of healthy mayonnaise
- If you need to increase your portions for more guests, add one egg or one tablespoon of mayonnaise for each guest

This is a fantastic meal on top of salad or vegetables. Consider color as you make this recipe your own.

And don't forget the leftovers! I had a terrific lunch recently of leftover carne asada with rice and beans. It was delicious, nutritious, and economical.

Feel free to include fruit with any meal. Its natural sweetness will curb your cravings for sweets, and will also speed up your metabolism. Fruit is a win-win food.

Another vital component of eating the foods that love you back is to drink a lot of water throughout the day. Water keeps you hydrated, which is essential to your health and wellbeing.

What about snacks?

Snacks are wonderful! Remember, this is not a program that is meant to deprive you when you feel hungry. Here are some awesome snack ideas for when you get the munchies between meals:

- Raw almonds (or any type of nuts without added salt)
- Apples
- Pears
- Bananas
- Watermelon
- Raisins
- Goat yogurt
- Hard-boiled egg

- Raw veggies
- Fresh strawberries with sour cream

So if you find yourself drained of energy but you still have two hours left at work, try a handful of almonds. Their crunchy goodness will perk you up and give you the energy you crave to finish off your day strong.

Juicing is also a terrific option. Mix up some veggies, fruits, or a combination of both, add some fiber, and you have a great pick-me-up between meals. This is especially useful on weekends when you have more time to get creative.

A DATE FOR YOUR DATE

ooooooooooooooooooooooooooooooooo

Now that you are eating the foods that love you back, I can't resist sharing a special dating tip.

Before your first date, eat three to five dates.

Why?

You will feel relaxed.

You will feel energized.

You will feel focused.

Dates are wonderful foods that love you back!

ONE MORE!

ooooooooooooooooo

One more hint: Do your best to eat dinner before 7:00pm. If you are attending a late-night event and have no choice, try to give yourself two to three hours to digest before you go to bed. Or have fun—stay up late and dance to rev up your metabolism!

Keep in mind every day is a new day filled with new experiences. Be proactive as you move through life, and utilize your flexibility and personal freedom to make choices that help you take pleasure in life. Food is your friend. It fuels you for the challenges ahead, and is also a gift to your senses. Make the most of your relationship with food. Enjoy!

TAKE YOUR TIME

ooooooooooooooooooooooo

Time is another critical component of this program. In our fast-paced world, we tend to eat just like we do everything else; at a hundred miles an hour! This is not the best choice for our health.

We need to devote time to eating. The slower we eat, the quicker we obtain the results we seek. Trust me on this. When I stopped rushing and took the time to eat slowly and properly digest my meal, I found that my metabolism actually sped up. This has allowed me to keep an ideal weight for many years.

Take at least twenty to thirty minutes to eat breakfast, thirty to forty minutes for lunch, and forty to fifty minutes for dinner. You will notice a difference. This also gives you time to fall in love with food! When you eat the foods that love you back, you learn to love food and the life it brings you. Fall in love with food, and with life. That love will come back to you in equal proportions.

In addition, I would like you to pay attention to your eating environment. Many of us have developed bad habits in this area.

Here is a list of don'ts that will help you gain maximum enjoyment while you eat:

- Don't drive while you eat. It's messy, and there's almost no chance you will eat slowly.
- Don't talk while you eat. You may have conversations during meals with your loved ones, but digest your food first.
- Don't work while you eat. You'll never get those crumbs out of your keyboard!
- Don't stand up or walk around while you eat. This isn't the time for multitasking.
- Don't go to the drive through. It's a quick fix with no lasting results.

Eating is a stand-alone activity. Take time to savor it.

Snacks are different. It's okay to munch on some carrots while you're working, studying, or doing house chores, or even stop for a snack while you're on a road trip. You need refueling as often as your car! But save some stand-alone time for your main meals. Food is that important.

Eating the foods that love you back and taking the time to do so is the first step on the ladder of success. You are building a solid, happy relationship with the thing that sustains your life.

This will soon translate into improved relationships with you, those around you, time, money, and exercise. Food will start you on the journey to balancing your life and promoting the lifestyle you desire.

LET FOOD COLOR YOUR LIFE

ooooooooooooooooooooooooooooooooooooooooo

There are many beautiful varieties of food. Take pleasure in the color spectrum available when you walk into your local market. Nature has quite a color palette!

When you include various colors of food into your daily diet, you are introducing an equal variety of nutrients into your body. Each color represents a valuable nutrient that exists only in that particular food. Color your world!

Imagine how each one of these beautiful colors goes to work building and fortifying healthy connections throughout your body. You will feel a difference in a matter of weeks.

NEVER ONE SIZE FITS ALL

ooooooooooooooooooooooooooooooooooooo

I have mentioned this previously, but I want to emphasize the point that we are not one size fits all. Each of us has our own preferences in all aspects of life, and food is not an exception.

That is one of the reasons I found specific diets frustrating. The types of foods that I love are different from the kinds of foods another person loves. It's that simple. Do the research. Take the three steps of this process seriously and determine from the vast color palette of foods which ones you like the most. Then enjoy them!

We must tune in to the foods that love us back and incorporate them into our day-to-day lives.

The more I practice this kind of food discovery, the more my tastes shift throughout the journey of my life. I encourage you to be bold and honor your unique tastes.

Change is constant, and so will be your choices of food. This is the spice of life! Practice getting out of the box and feel the liberation of befriending foods in a simple way.

IT'S ALL ABOUT RELATIONSHIPS

oooooooooooooooooooooooooooooooooooooooooo

As you practice this program you will find that food is a wonderful life teacher. It illustrates the simplest path to common sense, moderation, and creativity.

When we eat five bananas for breakfast, or three cheeseburgers for lunch, or two full salmon dinners, we are in a destructive relationship with food. We are in an irrational relationship with food! We are acting on emotions and ignoring common sense. This is dangerous. It impacts our health, finances, peace of mind, and our relationships with others. When we overdo it, we alienate ourselves from those around us.

Instead, let's celebrate our relationship with food and examine how healthy eating influences the other relationships around us. Food should be celebrated, honored, and appreciated for its life-giving properties. Not abused, neglected, or overused.

It's all about relationships. When we have a destructive relationship with food, the negative effects reach out in all directions:

- We lack energy
- We lose passion for life
- We lack enthusiasm
- We fall into the habit of hurting ourselves in other ways
- We have trouble focusing
- We have mood swings
- We don't produce in the workplace
- We don't take pride in our appearance
- We start to develop serious health issues (diabetes, heart problems, obesity, anorexia, bulimia)

This downward spiral does not discriminate. It hits people of a variety of ages, financial backgrounds, cultures, genders, and social levels. When we have a bad relationship with food, we can't avoid unhappiness. We attempt to hide it, but it's physically and emotionally impossible.

I can tell you this firsthand. I paid a pretty high price emotionally and physically for my bad relationship with food, but I am so grateful I woke up one day. Somewhere deep inside I found the desire and determination to make a change. I learned to love myself enough to transform my relationship with food from negative to positive. Now, it's my desire to help as many people as I can.

NOW WE HAVE 4 P'S

ooooooooooooooooooooooooooooo

The entire program of learning to eat the foods that love you back is based on 4 P's (you'll recognize three of them from earlier pages):

1. **Passion**. Love what you eat, and let it love you back.
2. **Preparation**. Take time to shop around and prepare key ingredients that will nourish you and make you feel great. Think color.
3. **Portion**. Remember to maintain reasonable portions. Overeating never feels good.
4. **Priority**. Give meals priority in your life. Never rush through them.

Start this program five days a week, and soon it will become a complete weekly program that you will absolutely love to follow.

You deserve to live life in vivid and beautiful color. Whether you are sailing a boat or sitting in a cubicle; driving a bus or running a law office; teaching school children or working in a doctor's office, this program is for you.

Your first step to a healthy, happy, and prosperous life is your relationship with food. You deserve to eat the foods that love you back. Love yourself enough to nourish yourself with great food. It's a two-way street. Once you start down this road, you will never go back.

> *If we're not willing to settle for junk living,*
> *we certainly shouldn't settle for junk food.*
> —Sally Edwards

Practice connecting your heart with your common sense and soon you will become an expert at balancing the two. Good choices are based in love, and are built one step at a time.

When you take hold of this program and make it your own, you will notice that you never have an empty stomach, and surprisingly, your bank account might start to become full. You will stop throwing away food that doesn't satisfy you, and you will also shed emotional weight.

Imagine opening your refrigerator door to view a less cluttered and friendlier variety of foods, a wide spectrum of natural colors to tempt your eyes and your stomach.

No matter how far technology has brought us, we still need to get back to basics if we want to survive. Food is necessary for life. If we learn to add a dash of love into our daily diet, we will uncover that happy balance between emotions and logic that generations have struggled to find.

Just listen to your body, eat in silence and see what feels good and you will spontaneously choose the foods that are beneficial to you.
—Deepak Chopra

Start with colorful, natural food. It's that simple. The rest will follow.

Today, I am happily married. I eat the foods that love me back, and I'm open to new experiences every day. I feel fueled and ready to go, no matter what life throws my way. My refrigerator and freezer are always at least fifty percent full. My pantry is stocked with mostly healthy and nutritional products. And once a day I indulge in a decadent piece of dark chocolate. It surely loves me back!

Remember, the special ingredient is a dash of love. It will color every aspect of your life.

YOUR PERSONAL FOOD LOG

ooooooooooooooooooooooooooooooooooooooooooo

On this and the following page, you will find a sample chart to list your progress. This will help you track what you eat and how your energy level, mood, and focus change. You will have an opportunity to rate your success on a scale of 1 to 5: 1 meaning "I rock!" and 5 "not so great."

I suggest you wait until the end of the day to rate your energy, mood, and focus, but keep these charts nearby throughout the day to accurately record the food you eat.

Meals I Had Today

My energy today was:

Excellent	Good	So-So	Weak	Blah
1	2	3	4	5

My mood today was:

Excellent	Good	So-So	Weak	Blah
1	2	3	4	5

My focus today was:

Excellent	Good	So-So	Weak	Blah
1	2	3	4	5

DON'T SWEAT IT

ooooooooooooooooooooooo

Do you have a gym membership? When was the last time you went?

After discussing food and energy level you probably had an inkling that I would move on to exercise. I can almost hear you groan. "Not again!"

Is exercise the first thing you drop when life gets busy? Maybe you'll get back on that treadmill as soon as you land the next business deal, or after your son's baseball season is over.

I know it's tough to find time to exercise. We have full lives and various commitments. We'll discuss time in the next section; so you have an opportunity to plan a time for exercise. But right now I want to address something basic. A lot of us think *exercise* is a bad word. Let's face it, we can't stand it.

This is where your mind shift comes in. Why do you bother? Because exercise is one of those ribbons that ties you to something you want, a healthier, happier life.

Now, let's rethink this whole idea....

The key is to find a type of exercise you enjoy. Whether it's walking, playing basketball, riding a bike, running, yoga, or another activity, experiment with the possibilities and then choose an exercise option that brings you joy.

It's outdated to think you will only reap benefits of exercise if you feel the burn and sweat for at least an hour. If you don't enjoy that, don't do it! Go for a walk in a nearby park with your partner instead. If you make time for that three times a week, you will not only derive the physical benefits, but you will also enjoy some quality time with the person you love. It's a great way to unwind at the end of a long day; or an early morning walk might be a pleasant way to ease into your day.

Exercise does not have to hurt. It can be truly enjoyable. Many people find yoga practices to be both relaxing and invigorating. Yoga also integrates meditation techniques that reenergize your mind, body, and spirit.

On the other hand, some of us enjoy the challenge of pushing our bodies to a new level. If that appeals to you, consider creating a goal by signing up for a half marathon in a city you have never visited. Training is enjoyable when a vacation is the final reward. And how great would it feel to accomplish something you have never done before?

At a minimum, try to carve out two to three hours a week to engage in exercise. You don't have to limit yourself to one type of exercise, either. Switch it up, if you like a little variety. You will notice a difference in your energy level and your attitude. If you really have a hard time getting started, find a friend who will exercise with you. Accountability is a wonderful tool to get you moving in the right direction.

There is a reason there are so many magazine articles, TV segments, and classes devoted to exercise. It has an incredible effect on your quality of life. Exercise reduces stress, diminishes anger, releases powerful endorphins, and gets you into the NOW. It feels good to participate in life.

LEARN TO LOVE MONDAYS

ooooooooooooooooooooooooooooooooooooooo

Another energy sapper I discovered is our attitude toward certain days of the week. Monday has had a bad rap for quite some time. Have you ever wondered why it's the least favorite day of the week?

Here are some questions to ponder:

- Why do people resent Monday?
- Why do most people dread going to work on Monday?
- Why is production and work efficiency rated the lowest on Monday?
- Why do so many people have low energy and bad attitudes on Monday?
- Why do people choose not to close deals on Monday?
- Why do people avoid going out on first dates on Monday?

There is a single, powerful answer to all these questions:

Monday marks the end of fun on the calendar.

Monday is the first day of the work week, which means responsibilities are back in full gear. The weekend is traditionally filled with enjoyable activities, but Monday is a return to the real world and the accountability that goes along with it.

People have difficulty switching from their carefree weekend attitude to the weekday blues. It's an emotional shift that feels like eating your vegetables.

I have always loved Mondays. (I like vegetables, too, but that's another story.)

Why?

I made a conscious choice to understand, appreciate, and welcome the first work day of the week. I feel enthusiastic about starting the week; it's my chance to get ahead, accomplish things, and produce results. Monday introduces a fresh, new color into my world. It's a new attitude, the freedom to choose to pursue my goals for the week at work and at home.

That simple shift in thinking has had a profound influence on my life.

For many years, I worked in the manufacturing industry. I have completed intensive research on productivity levels and employee attitudes toward Mondays. It was a surprise to me to learn that most people detest Mondays.

When I would call a business contact on a Monday, I could hear their lack of energy and enthusiasm over the phone. In fact, some of my colleagues shared their views on Mondays when I questioned them.

"How are you?" I would ask.

Here are some of their responses:

"I will be better on Thursday."

"It's Monday. What do you expect?"

"I wish it was still the weekend."

"I wish we could skip Monday and go straight to Tuesday."

Other comments uniformly followed that line of thinking.

Well, I thought to myself, if we skipped Monday, Tuesday would become the most unwelcome day of the week.

Regardless, people have a hard time breaking away from the weekend. The weekend was fun, free, a time to do anything they wanted to do. Monday is back to reality, papers piled up on your desk, chores at home, traffic, getting the kids to school on time, grocery shopping, preparing meals, taking kids to soccer practice and ballet lessons, cleaning the house, finishing a report for the boss and the list goes on … oh, if it was only Saturday again.

Stress replaces liberty.

Tasks replace time off.

Tedium replaces creativity.

That is what most of us think.

I would like to turn that mindset around. I can think of numerous reasons why Monday is a fabulous and important day of the week. It's time to ditch Monday's bad reputation and give it a new image.

When we choose to have a positive attitude about Monday, everything around us will begin to shift. Stress will be replaced by passion. We will have new energy and start feeling good about ourselves and our accomplishments early in the week. When we make this shift, we become better partners; more patient parents; more productive workers; and most significantly, we become stronger time managers.

On top of all that, we actually start enjoying what we do— even on Monday. We welcome responsibility, since we realize the opportunity to make things happen. We increase our success, make more money, and ultimately are rewarded by having more freedom. We will have new opportunities to travel, buy certain gadgets we want, and spend more time with family and friends.

When we make good use of Mondays, we stop carrying stress through the days of the week. We solve problems as they occur rather than putting them off, and we learn how to maximize every day of the week.

FUNDAY?

ooooooooooooo

I call Monday Funday. Don't laugh! It changes attitudes.

I must share a Monday morning event I introduced at one of the companies where I worked as an executive.

I decided to wait by the main entrance on a gloomy Monday morning and greet all the employees entering the facility. I smiled at them and announced, "Welcome, happy Monday to you!"

They looked at me as if I was insane. My cheery greeting didn't remove their frowns. Most mumbled a quick "good morning" and shuffled through the doors with zero enthusiasm.

After I had greeted about a dozen people, I came to the conclusion that I needed to do something about the bad attitudes in our organization. I knew it was affecting our bottom line. Our nightshift assembly line workers had to troubleshoot added issues due to problems the dayshift employees passed on to them on Mondays. Additional time was wasted on quality control and customer returns.

Monday was a low shipping day and a low point in the quality of our work. No one was in top form on Monday—they were all just waiting for the day to end.

As I stood in the doorway on that rainy Monday, a tremendous idea came to my mind.

I walked to the parking lot toward the next group of people locking their cars, and I asked them to walk back to their respective cars.

"Why?" they asked.

My answer was simple: I wanted them to start over with a fresh attitude. The moment they locked their car doors, I asked them to also lock away their weekend and bad attitude about Mondays. I encouraged them to turn around with a smile and walk toward the building with purpose—excited to be part of an organization that produced items that improved people's lives.

I thought if I could change the attitudes of a few employees, it would have a domino effect. We had to change our attitudes toward Mondays. It was as simple as that.

Again, they looked at me like I was insane, but they followed my instructions. I repeated this practice for several weeks, and attitudes began to change. Monday became a great day of productivity, shipping was up, and the company embarked on a whole new journey.

It wasn't just attitudes that changed, employees saw tangible benefits as a result of their new outlook. Management began to award quarterly bonuses as a result of increased revenue. They also decided to give every employee their birthday off with pay.

My "Monday is Funday" attitude was contagious, and I have introduced Happy Monday policies with countless organizations and individuals over the years.

The surprising success of this simple attitude change inspired me to design and create an easy, effective, and enjoyable Happy Monday program.

HAPPY MONDAY PROGRAM

ooooooooooooooooooooooooooooooooooooooo

As part of my Happy Monday Program, I introduce a short, motivational tip every Monday. The tips are in alphabetical order, we start with A, and when we get to Z, we begin again at the top of the alphabet.

My Happy Monday tips have been embraced by people and companies worldwide.

Corporations can launch these valuable tips in various ways:

- As a subtitle to their logo
- On business cards
- In fortune cookies
- Wrapped in chocolates
- On beverage containers
- On packaged foods
- On cell phone applications

The possibilities are endless.

Go confidently in the direction of your dreams!
Live the life you've imagined.
—Henry David Thoreau

I am delighted to share my Happy Monday tips. When you institute them into your daily life, you will enjoy the entire week. You will never have a blue Monday again.

In ninety to one hundred eighty days, you will not only embrace Mondays, but will also learn to let go, and enjoy the process of reaching your goals, and mastering the three crucial areas in your life:

1. Health
2. Relationships
3. Money

You will reduce stress and replace it with a zest for life.

Furthermore, in the event you are interested in taking the Happy Monday program a step further, I would be delighted to introduce to you the **Happiness Thermometer** course. Keep that in mind as you embark upon the journey to happy Mondays.

HAPPY MONDAY TIPS

ooooooooooooooooooooooooooo

A. **Acknowledge** the day. Greet your family members, coworkers, and others with a smile.

Add a positive attitude to your day. Your attitude sets the mood for the entire week.

Apply yourself. Focus on today. Your productivity will shine.

B. **Be** good to yourself. Treat yourself to something special, or take time to enjoy a special moment.

Be kind to others.

Be calm. Take three minutes every morning for a breathing exercise. Inhale and exhale slowly and steadily.

C. **Call** your friends, family members, co-workers, and other important people in your life. Reach out and let your voices connect.

Care to be your best when performing your daily tasks and responsibilities.

Chic achieves. Dress for the job you want rather than the one you have. When you look successful, you will become successful.

D. **Do** the things you need to do today, refrain from postponing difficult tasks.

Drink water throughout the day. It will energize you.

Dust off your weekend events. Introduce beauty and newness to every day of the week.

E. **Entertain** happy thoughts throughout the day.

Enjoy your first day of the week.

Enthusiasm is a powerful tool to celebrate your first workday of the week.

F. **Funny** quotes and jokes will enhance your day.

Flowers color your workplace.

Form your goals for the day.

G. **Go** forward with your goals.

Gain confidence and act accordingly.

Give time to your loved ones.

H. **Have** a clear plan for the week.

Honor and appreciate your work.

Hugs are important. Give and receive them often

I. **I** validate how others feel.

I feel love and gentleness in my heart.

I filter my words before I speak.

J. **Jump** into the day with both feet.

Jogging is great exercise. Give it a try.

Jobs are out there. Seek them with an open mind and a generous heart.

K. **Kindness** is in your nature. If it has slipped away, try to find it.

Kisses will light up your heart, soul, and body.

Keys open doors. Use them wisely.

Knowledge is a treasure. Apply it.

L. **Love** is a necessary ingredient in your life.

Laugh often. Laughter will lift your spirits.

Learn from experience, and teach others.

M. **Moms** are special. Appreciate them.

Motivate yourself. Motivation begins with you.

Mind your mind.

My grandfather's famous words: "What the mind cannot do, time can."

N. **Name** it. Say your name clearly and enthusiastically. It carries your reputation.

Newness is all around you. Monday is the introduction of a new week. Embrace it.

No is a powerful word. Use it with care.

O. **One** idea, one thought, one action can change the course of your life. Observe the power of one.

On and off switch determines your outlook. Turn on your positive button, and turn your negative button off.

Open the door to your Happiness. You have the power to do this.

P. **Passion** is a vital for motivation.

Pro-act when faced with a challenge and resolve it with confidence

Planning for tomorrow is good, but acting today is necessary.

Q. **Quality** is your friend.

Quantity is simply more, not always better.

Questions will lead to knowledge, understanding, and comfort. Ask questions.

R. **Respect** the feelings of others.

Remember to remember. Past experiences are a vast part of your personal growth.

Responsibilities keep us grounded.

S. **Set** your goals for the week. Then, attend to them.

Space and time are important. Allow space and time prior to acting on the choices you make.

Say it the way you'd like to hear it.

T. **Time** is a precious commodity. Befriend time, appreciate time, and use your time wisely.

Teach others. Take time to share your experience, understanding, and wisdom with others.

Trust that you don't need to know everything.

U. **Umbrellas** will protect you in the rain and from the sun. They are simple and practical inventions.

Unique. Everyone is unique. When you meet people, it's important to be interested rather than interesting.

U-turns will slow your success. Be aware of them, and watch your steps, so you can avoid the next U-turn.

V. **Values** define you.

Visiting a relative or friend is wonderful. Do not overstay your welcome.

Voices are meant to be heard. Speak out and speak up for yourself.

W. **When** I get this, when I get that, or when I get there, I will be happy. Life has countless destinations. Enjoy the stations in between.

Walking is great exercise.

Water is good for you. Drink it.

Weather is unpredictable. Don't imitate its dismal moods.

Will things to happen in your life. When there is a will, there is a way.

Work is the remedy for the ailments that hold you back from success.

X. **Xerox** is a patented process for copying documents. Don't copy others, be an original.

X it out. If something is not working, X it off your list and move on.

Xenolith is a rock fragment embedded inside another rock. It reminds us to make time for closeness and intimacy.

Y. **Yes** is a powerful word. One yes will change the course of your life.

Your attitude will change the course of your day.

Yellow is a happy color. Paint at least one wall yellow in your home. It will bring in the sunshine.

Z. **Zenith** is your highest point. Have you reached your zenith?

Zest for life is a necessary ingredient for a happy and fulfilled existence.

Zone out. Occasionally, you need a break. But don't forget to come back to the now.

Zip codes mark your geographic location. Get out and experience something new.

Zealousness is catching. Use your zealousness to inspire and energize others.

TAKE ACTION

ooooooooooooooooooo

Now that you have tips to inspire you on your journey to happier Mondays, it's time to roll up your sleeves and get some work done. Do you have an action list for the week?

Start working on it today. When you solidify your priorities in black and white, you have a greater chance of accomplishing them.

What better day to attack your action list than your new favorite day, Monday? Learn to love Mondays for the opportunities, challenges, and inspiration they bring.

My wish for you is a lifetime of Mondays filled with joy and action. When you embrace Mondays, you embrace life in all its beautiful colors.

On the next few pages, you will find sample charts to create your action items. Once they are completed, measure your success on a scale of 1 to 5.

Excellent	Good	Needs Improvement		Weak	Needs Work
1	2	3		4	5
Action List - Personal					
Item			Ranking		

Excellent	Good	Needs Improvement		Weak	Needs Work
1	2	3		4	5
Action List - Work					
Item			Ranking		

Excellent	Good	Needs Improvement		Weak	Needs Work
1	2	3		4	5
Action List – School					
Item			Ranking		

Excellent	Good	Needs Improvement	Weak	Needs Work
1	2	3	4	5
Action List - Home				
Item		Ranking		

Now you have a host of new tools to reignite your passion, shift your energy to the positive side, and embrace a happier attitude toward life. Tap into the energy available to you by using these tools, and watch how your increased energy changes your life and the lives of those around you.

Our essential ingredients to create 360° of success in life are almost complete. Time is the final ingredient.

PART IV

TIME—IT'S TICKING

The most important ingredient in this entire 360° of success is TIME.

TIME = LIFE

Without time, nothing happens. Time is the one thing we cannot trade, modify, or stop.

Sadly, we often misuse our time and realize too late that it slipped through our fingers. Time moves swiftly. We cannot turn back the clock, but we can take hold of this precious commodity, use it wisely, and appreciate every minute we are granted.

Let's explore how you can harness your time and maximize this valuable resource.

Time is our one constant companion in the journey through life. And just like we have developed a relationship with money and energy, we must also make friends with this traveling companion.

Sometimes we flow happily along with it, while other times we struggle against it. In reality, we don't struggle with time itself. We struggle with the things that prevent us from flowing with time.

We must make time our friend, because traveling with a friend is always better than traveling with a stranger; or worse, an enemy. We flow with time when time is our friend.

Time is our friend when we have the four P's of **passion**, **priority**, **portion** and **preparation.** When we flow easily with time, everything else comes together.

You have already been working on your relationship with time in the previous three sections. Now we will deepen our relationship with time through a few additional tools. Let's start with arresting the time thieves.

ARREST THE TIME THIEVES!

ooooooooooooooooooooooooooooooooooooo

Tricky time thieves hide among necessary and important activities. Wearing numerous disguises, they infiltrate our noble pursuits and dreams of living good and rewarding lives.

Two main keys will help you arrest the time thieves:

- Moderation
- Common Sense

This is all you need when you are ready to stop being a slave to time and start kicking the time thieves out of your life. If it was that simple, none of us would struggle with time. The real problem is time thieves wear disguises. We don't always recognize them when they appear in our lives.

Let's identify some of their sneaky disguises:

Relationships

Relationships should be nourishing to both participants. But the wrong relationship or the wrong approach to the right relationship steals your time. When you dwell on relationships in counterproductive ways your energy is depleted as well.

Do your part to maintain a healthy relationship. Use the tools you developed in Section II. Avoid negative time thieves that poke their ugly heads into your relationship; from impulses to crowd the other person to fixating on what is missing in the relationship. Negativity isn't just a time thief; it will damage your relationship. When you discover yourself in this situation, take a step back and refocus your attention.

This does not mean that you suppress conflict. Suppressing conflict is a definite way to destroy a relationship. Rather, when you have a conflict, deal with it. Work it out in a way that doesn't trample goals or self-esteem. Resist personal attacks, instead work together to identify and resolve the underlying issue.

For example, instead of dumping a bucket of negativity on the other person with a phrase like, "What a stupid idea!" respond with something like, "That's a very creative approach, but I have some concerns about [list concerns]. Can we work together about how to resolve them?"

Health

Too much attention to health concerns can steal your time; especially if you focus on the ailment and not the means to restoring your health. Did you know that when you react to perceived aches and pains, you can actually damage your health? When pain is your focal point, your body begins to regard pain as its natural state. This pilfers valuable time from improving your overall health status.

Remember that moderation is the key. Acknowledge your feelings about your health concerns and take positive steps to improve your condition. However, keep in mind that some things are beyond your control, and others are trivial in the big picture. Be proactive. Focus on the concerns you can easily affect, like eating well and getting enough exercise.

Nineteenth-century American humorist and lecturer Josh Billings said, "There are lots of people in this world who spend so much time watching their health that they haven't the time to enjoy it." Spend your time achieving health, not watching it slip away.

Fighting Our Nature

Trying to change your basic nature is difficult at best, and struggling against your nature is a misguided misuse of time. You can't change who you are. But you *can* change what you do, and that changes how you think and feel. First, determine what you can realistically change and accept what you cannot. Apply the changes in small steps, and be enthusiastic about your progress. Changing what you do in achievable ways will bring about new opportunities that will enrich your life.

Here's a simple mantra to keep you on the improvement path: *Stop trying to fight your nature; negotiate with it instead!*

Multitasking

A great American proverb states, "If you can't ride two horses at once, you shouldn't be in the circus." In our complex world, we are often required to multitask, but multitasking taken to the extreme becomes a time thief. Oftentimes, when we try to do more we actually accomplish less. Multitasking is effective when you properly balance all of the tasks. But unless you attain that balance, some or all of the tasks get shortchanged.

Learn the proper balance and make sure not to spread yourself too thin. We need to recognize when we have too much on our plate. Saying no is often the fastest and easiest way to recapture lost time. Seek help when you are overwhelmed. When you have extra time proactively assist others who have helped you.

Perfectionism

Efficiency expert W. Edwards Deming famously said, "The perfect is the enemy of the good."

We only need to be perfect in a few of the things we do. If you're performing heart surgery, piloting an airplane or performing a duty where lives depend on your flawlessness, strive for perfection. For most tasks, perfectionism is a time thief. While it's important to do your best, it is more important to recognize when the cost of doing more; in money, time, or stress exceeds its value. Acknowledge and understand when perfectionism is stealing your time. Then refocus your attention. Use your common sense to determine what truly needs to be perfect and what is good enough. Most things only need to be good enough!

Worry and Fear

Replace worry and fear with positive action, and you will regain large portions of time! A proactive approach goes a long way toward easing the underlying concern. Acknowledge and accept your fears; the calmer you are, the better you'll handle the real issues.

Remember: Most of the things you worry about never come to pass. Focus on productive use of your time, knowing that time and a positive approach will resolve many issues.

Anger

Anger is a particularly malignant time thief. Learn to replace time stolen by anger with positive action. If something is wrong in the world, organize a campaign to rectify it. If something is amiss in a relationship, have a nonjudgmental heart-to-heart talk. If he or she responds in anger, use strategies to validate their concerns while defusing their hostility.

Worry and anger are learned behaviors. When you focus on ways you can make the world, your neighborhood, or even your home a happier place, you prevent anger from stealing your time. However, if anger is a constant time thief in your life or if your safety is endangered by someone else's anger seek help.

Blame and Judgment

Blaming or judging others never solves anything. Shift your thinking, and examine the underlying issues that foster your defensiveness. Instead of blaming someone else take personal responsibility to resolve the problem.

Envy

Acknowledge and accept your feelings. There is no point in dwelling on why other people are obtaining things you think you deserve. Rather, seek to understand how they achieved this, and how you can too.

Wasting Time

You can never regain a wasted hour. Be mindful of how you spend your time and what it costs you to waste it. Set up systems to stay efficient. For example, keep articles where they belong, that way you don't waste time looking for something, because you know exactly where it is. Learn to hit the ground running when you start a new task or project. Don't squander time warming up.

Build time to decompress. The time you spend walking in the woods, meditating, reading a good book, cooking a nice meal, or listening to music is not wasted; it's essential!

Important Note about Unproductive Habits

You are in the process of changing a lifetime of poor habits. Don't expect to master the new strategies instantly. The changes to your core personality will be gradual. It took years to learn negative thinking and behaviors; replacing them will take time. But you can start right away.

Be conscious of times when you slip into your old, unproductive habits. Then shift your thinking and your behavior. Dump the useless habits and spend your time on productive activities. Each time you stop a negative thought or action pattern, you've won a victory.

RECLAIM YOUR TIME

ooooooooooooooooooooooooooooo

The Time Solution Formula below will support you with minimizing unproductive behaviors that steal your time. Immediately, you'll start to reduce their power over you; eventually, you'll eliminate these actions from your life. Identifying and eliminating unproductive behaviors will go a long way toward reducing their impact on your life.

The Time Solution Formulas allow you to control of your time. You will become more productive, experience less stress, and enjoy more fun. Every time you apply the formula, you're arresting another sneaky time thief.

The success of this formula requires feedback. Complete the form below every week. It will help you confront and defeat the time thieves by keeping track of how much time they have stolen from you. Equally important, you also track the time you recapture. Once you've used the chart below for a few weeks, you will readily spot areas for improvement. You'll rapidly gain more control of your time. Congratulations! You are no longer a slave to time.

Week:	S	M	T	W	T	F	S	Σ
Stolen Time								
Time Thieves								
Relationships								
Health								
Fighting our nature								
Multitasking								
Perfectionism								
Worry								
Anger								
Fear								
Blame & Judgment								
Jealousy								
Unproductive Habits								
Wasting Time								
Total Lost Hours								
Recovered Time								
Additional Activities								
Total Recovered Hours								

Time Balance								
Net Lost or Recovered Hours								
Notes								

TIME SYSTEMS

ooooooooooooooooooo

The Time Systems is your personal guide for shifting your life from overwhelmed and stressed to managed and happy. This is an additional tool to support you in managing your time to its maximum potential.

The Time Systems is a color coded chart, which will help you define your priorities. You will decide what goes into the chart, based on what is important to you. Then you choose your favorite colors to represent the items listed on your chart. The Time Systems chart will serve as a friendly reminder of what you need to do and what is important to you.

PERSONAL	EDUCATION	WORK/CAREER
Eat	Lectures	Email
Sleep	Read	Telephone
Exercise	Homework	Finances
Meditate	Essays	Filing
Finances	Test	Follow Up/Contracts
Health Care	Papers	Assignments
Personal Care	Group Study	Meetings

As you build your chart, you choose your own categories, activities, and colors. Here is an example:

FAMILY	HOUSEHOLD
Communicate	Cleaning
Follow Up	Laundry
Get Together	Cooking
Homework Kids	Gardening
Shopping	Organizing
Entertainment	Shopping
Emotional Support	Baking

SOCIAL	HOBBY
Music	Travel
Dancing	Arts
Get Together	Cooking
Entertaining	Gardening
Entertainment	Reading
Intimacy	Music
Support/Friends	Invent

The colors you pick for the chart will illustrate how your activities fit into categories. The next step is to use the colored items to prioritize your week.

SUN	MON	TUES	WED	THUR	FRI	SAT
Exercise	Email	Finances	Email	Follow Up/ Contracts	Filing	Intimacy
Cooking	Meetings	Telephone	Assignments	Email	Email	Shopping
Gardening	Telephone	Email	Cooking	Cooking	Telephone	Laundry
Homework	Cooking	Exercise	Cleaning	Exercise	Cooking	Cleaning
Entertaining	Read	Support/ Friends	Intimacy	Homework	Dancing	Baking

Feel free to email me for additional blank charts as free downloads. Please send your request to ana360degreecoach@gmail.com.

We all need simple, friendly tools to effectively build a relationship with the tasks we resent doing. Unfortunately, they don't disappear if we ignore them. This tool will help you see them clearly and get the jobs done. When we change our attitude about what we don't like doing, we change our personal relationship with things that block us from achieving success. The Time Systems method provides you a concrete way to pinpoint and act on those obstructions. You will then have a clear path for the things you really want to do.

TAKE A BREAK

ooooooooooooooooooo

Throughout this book I discuss numerous actions you can take to harness time, money, energy, and relationships in order to grow your personal and professional success. But there is one very important item that even a person with boundless resources has to remember, take a break!

We all must take breaks to recharge our minds and bodies. Breaks are essential fine threads that run through our lives. If they are not an important part of your routine, make a change today and incorporate them into your life. Breaks are critical to your health, happiness, and ultimate success.

There are a variety of ways to take a break. Some people enjoy simply chilling out and doing nothing; others like to meditate. Maybe taking part in an athletic activity gives you a break from your normal routine. Uncover what makes you happy, and honor it.

You do not have to constantly be on the move in order to achieve success. Down time is equally important when you are headed toward your ultimate life goals. It is essential to take time to recharge. Also, breaks from familiar routines reveal a different perspective to complete your 360° view. You will grow and change from the breaks you choose to give yourself.

I propose at least three types of breaks:

1. Every hour, take a three-minute break and simply do nothing. This connects you to the 3-Step/30-day program in the first phase.
2. At least a few times a week, take a longer break from your routine (at least 30 minutes) to do something you enjoy.
3. At least once a year, take a vacation away from home to unplug completely from obligations, recharge, and experience new things.

Breaks are as important to your success as any other suggestion in this book. You cannot lead a fulfilling life if you don't take regular moments to rest and revitalize.

NOW TIME WORKS FOR YOU

ooooooooooooooooooooooooooooooooooooooooo

Now you are in control! You have utilized tools that illustrate how you can maximize your time to its fullest potential. The next step is to turn the time thieves into employees. How will you plan your time wisely so your passions and success continue to grow? Time works for you now. It, too, has become your friend and ally.

LINKING IT TOGETHER

ooooooooooooooooooooooooooooooooo

You have done some incredible work as you navigated the pages of this book. I commend you for sticking with me to the end. Now you know my secrets! You are ready to assess and improve your life from every angle. You now have a 360° view of success and the tools to spiral higher than you have ever gone before.

To link these four important areas of Money, Relationships, Energy, and Time, start by remembering your passion seed. In the 3-Step/30-Day Program, you listed your dreams and goals. Take a look at them again. Now you can attain those dreams.

Let's review some takeaways from each of the four areas to complete your full 360° view:

MONEY
- Be passionate about money, but don't let it be your master
- Learn to portion your money and let it circulate
- Expedite money according to your priorities

- Maintain a healthy balance of income, expenses, and obligations
- Your business and personal wealth will grow if you utilize the 3 P's
- Let your money work for you
- Learn when to invest, when to spend, and when to give
- Ten minutes a day can turn your dreams into reality in the 3-Step/30-Day Program
- Concentrate on money flow, not money hold
- Work less and earn more with passive income streams
- Deepen your friendship with money
- Money alone will not buy happiness

RELATIONSHIPS

- We are not islands. Healthy business, personal, and family relationships are essential to a happy life
- Be more interested and less interesting
- Be passionate about people
- Good relationships reduce stress
- Remember the three secret formulas for creating a relationship
- Relationships are valuable commodities
- Flow through the five levels of relationships
- Great business relationships increase efficiency
- Stay focused in the chaos
- Alone time is important to recharge your batteries
- The sweets must exceed the crumbs in a personal relationship
- Keep track of your relationships. Nurture them and watch them grow

ENERGY

- Energy reignites your passion
- A positive outlook directly affects your energy level
- For increased energy, eat the foods that love you back
- Let good food color your life
- Try a cleansing event before changing your eating habits
- Experiment with the 3-Step/30-Day Method
- Develop a great relationship with food
- Now there are four P's: Passion, Preparation, Portion, and Priority
- Find exercise options you enjoy
- When you have positive energy, you are a magnet for people
- Detach yourself from negativity and manifest positive things in your life
- Break down tasks. It will increase your chances of accomplishing them
- Learn to love Mondays
- It's all about attitude

TIME

- Time is the most important area of 360° success
- Time=Life
- Beware of time thieves
- Moderation and common sense will improve your relationship with time
- Adjusting how you spend your time will not happen overnight
- Practice the Time Solution formula
- Utilize the Time Systems to shift your life from overwhelmed to content

- Don't waste time on things that give you nothing in return
- Find time to pursue your passion every day
- Learn to prioritize. It will open you up to living in the NOW
- Time must also become your friend

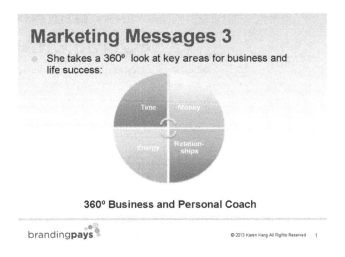

Money, **Relationships**, **Energy**, and **Time**—they come together beautifully to give you 360° of access to an abundant, happy, and successful life. You have seen that business, personal, and family aspects of your life are intertwined. The skills you have learned from these pages are designed to increase your awareness of how seamlessly they come together as you spiral up the circle of success.

I hope you take the information I have provided and run with it. Grab onto the life you want and enjoy every minute of it! I wish you overflowing success and happiness.

THE FINALE
BONUS CHAPTER

OOOOOOOOOOOOOOOOOOOOOOOOOOOOOOOOO

I magine a dining room table with 4 legs. In the event **that we pull away one** leg**; what happens to the table?** Can we place food and other accessories on it and sit comfortably? **No!** This is what the 4 components; money, relationships, energy, and time represent. They are connected and the 4 components work and sustain our lives just like the 4 legs of the table.

To keep the legs together and maintain the stability and the strength, we need to introduce a powerful and substantial foundation **(the table top)** so we can skillfully connect the existing components.

I am happy to introduce the finale to this book: **"The Ancient Wisdom of Hats; Switching the Roles in our Lives"**

This chapter will help us connect the 4 components: money, relationships, energy and time. Most importantly it will activate them with spirit, feelings and common sense. Ultimately you will reach your 360 degrees of success at home, at work, at school and everywhere else between your destinations.

THE ANCIENT WISDOM OF HATS SWITCHING THE ROLES IN OUR LIVES

ooooooooooooooooooooooooooooo

A Revolutionary Fictional Exercise
Providing Realistic Results

For the finale I will introduce to you the ancient wisdom of hats. What do they represent in our lives; and why is the shifting of hats program embraced by people from all walks of life? When we need to smoothly shift roles to meet life's demands we can utilize the metaphorical changing of hats to successfully master the skill of ...

Let's talk about hats in general. Why are they valuable and important in our lives? Hats protect us from getting sunburned, keep us warm, not to mention caps we use to play sports and helmets to protect us.

Before we move forward let's take a look back at the significance of hats in the 18th century. In the 18th century hats were:

- Fitted to reflect the status of the person who wore it by the form and shape of its design
- Used to signify a person's status in society, their gender and personal commitments
- Used to divide the seasons
- Employed via movement in accordance to various types of events

In the 18th century some of the "rules" of hat etiquette included:

Removing the hat was a sign of respect and recognition. One would take off his hat upon entering any home, a place of business, or a place of negotiation. Placing the hat back on the head signified closure to the connection and a simple good-bye. Upon entering a place of prayer, or the office of a recognized leader, the hat needed to be quickly removed and held in the right hand. When entering a home, the wearer would remove his hat instantly and place it in a safe, protected place in the entrance of the home.

Kings and queens wore elevated hats with jewels and precious stones. Their hats were usually dark purple, decorated with amethysts and blue sapphires. On special occasions, royalty wore crowns made of gold or silver layered with diamonds and precious stones. A regal young girl would wear a hat with lace around it as a symbol of purity, innocence, and availability. On special occasions, royalty wore pearl crowns with rubies or amethysts and round, blue sapphires. On average days, royalty would wear medium-sized hats made of the finest silk, decorated with multiple colored stones and small diamonds.

An impoverished man or woman wore a simple, dark, stiff wool hat. The poor would also lightly turn down the brim to cover the forehead and the face. It was a sign of weakness and complete humility.

Businessmen wore large brimmed hats with sharp, pointed fronts. This symbolized intelligence and a position of high esteem.

A young lady in search of a suitor wore a colorful hat, typically purple or blue, and thinly tailored in the back. A prominent married woman wore a round, full hat, usually black, brown, gray, or burgundy. The hat represented partnership and security. Children wore small, thin hats, designed in a square shape for protection, and as a representation of the learning ahead of them.

Teachers wore black hats as an emblem of authority, academic knowledge and supervision. People in the medical field wore dark green hats. They believed that green was the most pleasant color to observe, as it matched the color of outside greenery. Artists and musicians sported dark blue or dark purple hats made of shiny material, with a thin brim.

Gypsies and destitute people wore black, flat hats. The hats were made of thick rough wool and fit their heads completely, showing no brim at all.

Country people wore a light brown hat comprised of straw or leaves for the summer season. The hats were round and large to protect them from the sun. In winter to keep warm, they wore small hats made of sheepskin, with flaps and tied together under their chins.

Dancers and common girls available to be with anyone wore a bright red hat with colorful silk or shiny ribbons tied around the neck. The tie suggested they could be bought with goods or money.

Priests wore small hats, mostly of thick red wool, gathered in the middle and pointed. The height of the hat reminded the crowd that the clergy were centered and spiritually wise. In addition, these hats also symbolized that priests were extremely powerful and influential. The fabric gathered in the middle of the hat symbolically held them aloft from the general populace. The clergy were on a higher level, and they ruled with fear, judgment, and endless expectations.

Revolutionary or influential people wore gray hats with a black brim. The hats were thin and small, indicating the sharpness of their leadership. They were made with a diminutive slender cap in the front and flat in the back. Athletes wore the same type of hats in blue, brown, black, and rust.

Indeed, hats had something to say 200 years ago! They:

- Represented title and status
- Were created for fashion and clarity of status
- Fit the time, place and purpose of the message
- Were treated seriously, and with great respect
- Were a significant part of the clothing of the day

Now let me share the connection between switching roles/ switching hats and the 360 Degrees of Success Program. When we carefully adjust our roles we are automatically directed to our optimum personal and professional level. Ultimately we learn to enjoy the now (the hat we wear at the present time); we are completely focused and do what is expected. In the process we learn to reduce stress and overwhelming sensations. We implement the four ingredients into our daily lives. We understand why we wear a certain role at a particular moment. It is all interconnected from the outside in. The switching of the roles (hats) teaches us when to connect or disconnect in order to maintain a balanced and colorful life. This is the foundation to reaching your 360 degrees of success. The principles in this book represent the technical portion gearing you to The 360 Degrees of Success. The switching of the hats is filled with emotions, feelings and vulnerability. When these tools are linked we accomplish the goal.

Let me help you with the concept of the wearing of the mental hat. So let's open this chapter with some colors and what they represent.

White

The white hat is round and made of fine silk. Wear it at that peaceful place called home. Focus only on your home life and detach yourself from the outside world.

Red

The red hat is made of a thick ribbon silk, high and round in the front and square in the back. Wear the red hat when you are out having fun with friends or lovers. Red indicates passion, a break from routine. When you socialize be entertaining, light and exuberant. People love to be around energetic, fun, and charismatic personalities. Detach yourself from responsibilities and personal matters troubling you. Enjoy every second of your time wearing this hat.

Purple

The purple hat is sheer. It is clarity you are seeking, an understanding of your destination. Wear this hat when you are in a meditation mode, seeking intimate time with yourself. Don it during quiet times when you are one with yourself, not lonely, but alone. You need to detach yourself completely and stay put. Do this exercise three to four times a week, ten to fifteen minutes each time. The purple hat is a powerful yet calming color. It provides you the desire and strength to separate yourself from the outside world. To keep you centered you may choose to wear it at the park, on the beach, in the mountains, or even the desert.

Green
The green hat is made of thick wool, imparting financial strength and wisdom. Wear the green hat when conducting business or work. It is appropriate for all types of workers. Green represents the color of currency, abundance, and the respect for money. It also represents appreciation given to the customer. It shows you put a great deal of thinking into the products you sell or represent. Green also represents the experience and stability attained from understanding and focusing on your profession.

Blue
Wear the blue hat when you participate in an athletic activity. Blue is the color of the sky and the ocean. Water is endless, spectacular and always changing. Do not look at the winning moment; let your own journey move and flow. You can change within the game. Flow with it and the results will be rewarding. Blue also has a calming effect on us. Be centered, be calm, and do not feel anxious.

Blue is dynamic leadership. Oceans and rivers are in continuous motion. You wear the light blue hat when you drive a vehicle or pilot an airplane. Blue is the color of the sky on a clear day. You need to see the direction you take.

Black

Wear the black hat as a sign of respect for others during their difficult moments. As soon as you offer your respect remove it and replace it with the light blue one. This means you are once again in the driver's seat.

Yellow

Yellow is the color of the sun and moon. It lights the path and fills it with sunshine and warmth. Wear the yellow hat as a parent. As a parent, you need to exercise your knowledge and experience rearing your children. They require your guidance and expertise. Parents need to listen to the words between the lines and recognize how children react to voice tone, harsh words, punishment and loneliness. Children are influenced by their parents' behavior and approach to challenges. Social circles also influence your children's life as well as the environment at home. As a parent, you need to bring sunshine and warmth into your children's growth and upbringing. When you become a parent, your heart does get that special light—maintain it throughout your entire life. Once a parent you are always a parent.

Brown

Wear the brown hat when you are facing a stressful situation. You must be realistic when wearing this hat. Brown is the color of the frail leaves of autumn. They are weak and easily fall to the ground. The brown hat is a reminder of vulnerability. It represents the choice we need to make to be proactive in a stressful situation. It also validates other's needs and moments of weakness. You can fall down when you allow your ego to lead. Relinquish control, and the situation will become more in control. Brown is between black and other colors. You can choose the space in between and place the situation on hold for a while. Address challenges when the proper time comes.

Pink

Wear the pink hat when interacting with family members. Pink is a peaceful, pleasant color. It will reflect our behavior and approach to getting together with family. Often times family members lack chemistry and bring in the wrong energy. Some love to get into confrontations and arguments. Some love to compete and talk only about themselves, allowing their egos to run the show. At times family members feel distant to one another and this brings out their worst characteristics. By wearing the pink hat, you keep a certain peace when you get together. You feel uplifted, and you do not react to other family members' behaviors by placing more wood on the fire. You are content and keep on smiling. As we all know, we cannot change other's moods or personalities. Family get-togethers are very important and vital in keeping your own household together. Everyone can bear a few hours with relatives with whom they do not have the best connections. It's okay. The pink hat also represents short-term togetherness. The relatives will depart, or you will leave their house or place of gathering, and return home.

Wearing pink also teaches you how to introduce humor to the occasion—jokes, laughter and light, trivial conversation. When you bring that type of approach and behave calmly and pleasantly, you impact the rest of the family members. If they arrived with bitterness, anger, jealousy, and negative thoughts, the laughter and the jokes will diminish their strength and influence. For some people, this is easier than for others. They can behave diplomatically and respectfully, controlling how they feel about those family members. However, when the situation is unpleasant, that is when you have to remind yourself that you are wearing the pink hat and the situation is only temporary. The pink hat will bring out the best in you, and you will walk away less stressed. Social events and family gatherings are supposed to be enjoyable. You should not have to work hard to make it pleasant, and time will pass faster. It works for me, and believe me, every family has some people whom you rather not see at all. You can choose friends, but you cannot choose to belong to another family.

Multicolored

Wear your multicolored hat while on vacation. Blue, green, red and yellow are a good mix of colors. The multicolored hat is the symbol of being open-minded. Invite your vacation place into your album of experience. Become familiar with the place and enjoy every second of the experience. You are on vacation. Be completely there and stay in the moment. Explore the area; watch, listen and see the differences between the place you live and the vacation spot. Be friendly. Greet people with a smile. Sometimes we quickly bond with a new place, and at times it takes several days to become comfortable. Some people never feel right being in a new place. They imagined it; they planned on it, but when they got there, it seemed too far from their perception. When that happens remind yourself that you are wearing the multicolored hat. You will slowly adapt to the place, knowing that you are only there for a few days. Time is moving forward, you will be home in no time. Let go of your control and give yourself a chance to enjoy the experience. You are adding knowledge into your book of life. You are enriching yourself with this visit. If the place does not look or feel or represent everything you saw in the brochure, make the best of it. Do not fight with your feelings and disappointments. Take it easy. You are there already. See and examine what else is out there. Pick and choose. The worst that can happen is that you will not go back there again.

If the food does not agree with you, pick fruits, vegetables, bread, and cheeses, and eat what makes you feel right. Several times I went to a place and I thoroughly enjoyed myself, but the food did not agree with me. I went to the local grocery store and bought a few rolls, some butter, cheese, a few tomatoes, cucumbers, peppers, apples, and grapes. I ate that way for several days. My stomach was never empty, and I felt good. I wound up spending very little money on food.

You can make a new situation work in your favor by being open-minded, concentrating on the practical side of the matter, using your common sense, and extracting the experience from the adventure. When you visit a place with loved ones or you visit people you care about, your heart is filled with a loving connection. Give energy to that feeling. When you get home and flash back to the place you just left and develop your photographs, these bring a sharp recollection back into your mind, and you say to yourself, "I've been there, I know how it is there, I got to see the place," and then you can go back to your regular routine. Vacation is supposed to be a colorful experience.

Peach/orange

Wear a peach or orange colored hat when you shop. Think of an orange or a peach. It is pleasant to the eye. It is inviting. Peach and orange are the colors of the sun. We need the warmth and the brightness for shopping. You are about to spend some money for new things. You feel good when you see beautiful things for your home and you become creative in your mind. You can see how that particular vase or chair will look in your living room. When you shop for clothes for yourself, you gain confidence and recognition by observing yourself in the mirror. You look good. It fits you perfectly. Shopping for gifts provides a sense of giving and appreciation. Automatically we feel uplifted and enthused. The peach color warns us not to end up with a lemon when shopping. When you are out shopping for a major purchase, do your homework beforehand. Be intelligent and educate yourself. Take your time. Let time get your goals. Do not end up with a lemon of a purchase, because lemons will never be peaches. Bite into a peach, it will taste sweet and delightful. A lemon is sour when you squeeze it into your mouth. Just look into the mirror and see the difference.

Gray

Wear the gray hat when you need to make a decision. Remember a decision is not always black or white. Sometimes you are better staying put for a while. Do not make the decision too quickly. For certain circumstances or at certain moments in time, we need to wear the gray hat. We cannot be biased. There is a fine line between the extremes.

Let me give you an example. Many people are gifted, talented, and highly intelligent. They study a topic for many years. They become book smart. They learn the technical part of the data, the research, and the final outcome according to the literature.

Then they experience the reality of the situation. An architect, one of best in his class, builds an incredible high-rise building out of paper and aluminum using glue and other types of adhesive. He has never worked in the outside world. Now this architect is out in the job market. He has received an incredible offer, so he accepts. The very first project is a high rise building in a large city.

The weather there is humid, and it rains four to six months of the year. The city has also experienced earthquakes.

The architect quickly learns that it is not all about the books he read or the sample projects he did. He has to take other factors into consideration. So his design decisions are not truly black or white. You have to observe the in-between facts, and be flexible and open to understand the fine print in the gray areas.

Another example is of a teacher in a classroom. A teacher cannot approach each student in the same way, nor should she expect the same type of work from every student. The students are in the same class, but each one has their own personality. All students are products of their families, backgrounds, and social and economic situations. They have their own perceptions of things. Students react in different ways to new teachings. The teacher needs to analyze the gray area. She cannot be too structured or too set in ways. She presents the academic topic in one form, but she will also have to adapt to the learning styles of her/his students.

Gray represents clouds covering up the clarity. Gray teaches you how to appreciate and see clearly when the situation is resolved as well. Gray is also the color of fog. When you are driving and it's getting very foggy out there and you cannot see where you're going, you need to drive carefully. The road can be dangerous. What do you do? You stop and you wait patiently to allow some time for clearing up. Then you can pursue your mission afterward. Indeed, gray is the color of being alert, awake, and cautious about time.

Navy

Wear a white hat with navy blue stripes when you study or pray. Wear this hat when you are conducting a meeting, speaking in front of an audience, or presenting a product. Navy is a friendly business and professional color. It suits the occasion in a special fashion. It is not black nor is it light in color; it is midnight blue, the color of the sky at night. Navy blue is an inviting color, yet serious and respected. It is a clean color, and can be enhanced with other colors. It is very accommodating. Whites, powder blue, green, yellow, pink, beige, brown, purple, wine and even black all look right with navy. Imagine the sky at night. The stars shine like diamonds lighting up the sky. You can easily spot them on a clear night. A business presentation, a meeting, or a speaking engagement must show the foundation and the teachings for clarity and results.

Fuchsia

Wear a fuchsia hat when you dance, sing, listen to music, or just move to the rhythm. Fuchsia is full of nostalgia. You share your feelings with art and your creative side is flowing. Art brings out emotions, talents, and skills you never knew you had. You are completely detached from responsibilities and work. Art takes you to a fun place. Art is therapy. It is not an escape. Art expression, regardless to shape or form is a colorful break from tension, anxiety and stress. Art contributed to your AHAA moments!

Be an original

Wear a hat with multiple dots when making love. It sounds funny and eccentric. Your initial thought will be, *No hats!!* Well, have you ever found a rule prohibiting it? Making love is an art. Making love and being in love is getting out of your shell. You give yourself do not hold back. You are completely in the moment, detaching yourself from everything else. When you make love, you see the stars, the colors of the rainbow, and the sunlight coming into your soul and body at the same time.

Making love is the finest connection and bonding between two people. It is more than just the physical act, which can be an empty experience for both men and women. When an individual seeks only the physical satisfaction, he/she walks away with emptiness or the feeling of victory and triumph obtained from the experience. What happens then? You move on to the next one; ultimately you are alone.

I will compare it to something very simple. Take a clear glass and pour into it one drop of water or other type of drink. Let your partner pour in another drop of water, or other type of drink. What happens? They become one and you cannot separate them. That is what lovemaking can be all about. Two together become one in every way possible.

They are completely bonded and the time is speckled with dots, the symbols of the various feelings you are reaching and releasing at the same time. Considering everything else we do, we spend little time making love. Why not make it special, and unique. It is supposed to take you away from everything and allow you to be in the moment. The dots stand for the thin line between your background, your existence, your life and the main game you play.

Making love can always be a wonderful experience. Be considerate, be there for one another, and pick the right time when you can truly be in dots and not in doubt. Do not fear to make love. When we say the words "make love," we understand that we are making a work of art together and that the piece is perfect. Do not hold back. After making love, you feel not only refueled, relaxed, at ease, but you are in a complete state of detachment from stress.

Exercise, proper diet, lots of restful sleep, vacation time, and money, are important tools that add quality to our lives. Making love is all of the above in one drop. It is powerful. It is natural. It is complete giving and receiving. One needs to learn the skill of receiving; when you do, you know how and when to give. Time will be there for you. Just make time for it.

When traveling to a new destination how many times have you become lost or missed the exit? When you are lost put on your blue hat and:

Last Hat

I left one hat for last. When we feel beautiful, we want to look attractive. We put on our favorite clothes, shoes, and accessories. Let us also don a clear, see-through hat with light blue dots. This hat is clear so we can see through the entire exterior—we show the inner us—our character. Let us shine from within. We must be clear in our direction and purpose.

The light blue dots represent the challenge, the scale between good and evil; the temptation. The concentrations on materialistic things and appearance have become important factors in our modern lives. We fail to accept one important fact; it does not last. Things may keep you going for a while, but they cannot give you the strength you need at difficult moments.

See clearly and keep a sharp mind. Be strong and find the light within the commotion of life's events. Enjoy the now. Be good to yourself. Acknowledge the importance of others. Understand the reason for relationships and your time alone, the time between destinations, your goals, and your achievement of the mark.

Value your time. Cherish it and love it. You have the freedom to do whatever you want to do with it. Life is time, and time fills life. Love time and enjoy your life! Live in the now! Be a friend to stress, deal with it in the now, and move forward with your life.

The hats are a metaphor. They exist to help you balance the roles in your daily life. We cannot deal with everything we face in the same fashion, color, shape, or attitude.

Most importantly you need to learn to switch on and off the respective imaginary hats to release stress and to detach from clutter in your lives. Focus on the now—the role you are assuming at this very moment—and be the best that you can be. You will succeed and excel.

How do you learn to use time wisely, separate yourselves from emotional behavior, and search for facts and positive results? Only by living in the now and blocking out all other interruptions and disturbances. We cannot handle everything at once. Challenges will come and go, but change is always certain.

By practicing the formula with the "Ancient Wisdom of Hats," and embracing the colors, shapes, and textures you imagine, you will begin to love time.

You need to keep peeling off, and putting on your various hats to remind yourselves of the roles you play in your daily lives. You fulfill your expectations and your enthusiasm. Keep all of your hats clean. They need to stand out, and so do you.

By wearing the hats and detaching yourself from the outer circle, you can maintain a clear channel to stay in the moment. The results will be amazing. You will reduce your stress levels because you are dealing with one thing at a time. So get out there and detach yourself from the next project, the next meeting, and whatever else is preventing you from living in the now.

You wear multiple titles and roles within your lives, but you can become rich with wisdom and experience when you apply and practice this simple program. You will smile more often and be fulfilled.

Understand and accept changes, the highs and the lows of life, in their proper fashion. Do you remember the scale mentioned earlier? Life will always present the scale.

I have a short story to share with you.

A few years back, the corporation I was working for invited the management staff to a cruise on a lovely boat. It was in the middle of the summer, and the boat was cruising around San Pedro Harbor back to Marina del Rey.

We had a few refreshing drinks and a huge ice cream cake for dessert. It was a fun socializing time, and everyone was in a great mood, laughing, talking, and listening to music.

I was standing on the balcony when I noticed a large yacht cruising by. Two young girls were sitting on the deck sun tanning. They were already cocoa colored, and their white bathing suits contrasted sharply with their skin.

The boat sped off, and the foamy ocean waves cleared a powerful path to follow. That was when I noticed the large letters engraved in gold on the back of the yacht: WHAT'S NEXT!

It made me think. We entertain our minds continuously with the idea of what is next! Indeed, what is next can be sweet, exciting, and fruitful. In the meantime, however, be fulfilled and extract the wisdom of the now. Use the hats as profound metaphoric tools to connect you to common sense and tailor the wisdom to fit your needs and expectations.

We become happier people and we embrace life, all the "no's" in our lives teach us how to clean the soil and pursue the planting of new seeds – and that is what 360 degrees of success is all about.

As we masterfully practice the yin and yang life becomes colorful and meaningful, purposeful and full of passion. We become happier and embrace life's circumstances as a means of cleaning the soil and planting new seeds of experience and enthusiasm. This indirectly impacts the aging process. Billions of dollars are spent on anti aging products, services and teachings and yet it all comes down to one simple formula: Time equals Life.

The wisdom of switching hats will be tremendously instrumental and helpful when individuals switch from the army life to civilian life.

So to wrap it all up, we are in charge of our allotted time and the switching of hats connects us to the present time.

I am happy to take this opportunity to share these simple formulas. Please place them on the wall, refrigerator or anywhere you can see them and observe, absorb and practice.

- o TIME equals LIFE
- o LIFE equals TIME
- o ENERGY equals TIME multiplied by ACTION
- o ACTION equals RELATIONSHIPS plus MONEY multiplied by TIME
- o NO's equals LEARNING, AWARENESS, FOCUS multiplied by UNDERSTANDING
- o UNDERSTANDING multiplied by LISTENING and COMMON SENSE equals VALIDATION
- o LETTING GO plus DECLUTTERING equals THE NOW
- o THE NOW equals PLANTING NEW SEEDS equals ACTION
- o ANCIENT WISDOM OF HATS equals SHIFTING OF ROLES minus STRESS
- o STRESS REDUCTION equals BALANCE
- o BALANCE MONEY plus RELATIONSHIPS plus ENERGY plus TIME equals HAPPINESS

- ○ HAPPINESS equals HEALTH equals SUCCESS 360 DEGREES
- ○ 360 DEGREE SUCCESS equals FREEDOM
- ○ FREEDOM multiplied by TIME equals LIFE

Thank you for sharing.

Wishing you a tremendous successful life at 360 degrees.

Ana Weber

ANA WEBER IS THE
360° BUSINESS AND PERSONAL COACH.

Bestselling Author | Financial Turnaround Expert

Ana is a master at coaching entrepreneurs faced with challenging business issues.

Her simple and powerful approach to life and business is documented in her bestselling and inspiring books, *The Money Flow* and *Money, Relationships, Energy, Time: The Four Essential Ingredients for 360° Business and Personal Success.*

Ana progressed from being a penniless immigrant from Eastern Europe to starting over in Israel and the United States; eventually becoming a successful executive and entrepreneur.

She was instrumental in increasing a company's annual revenues of $250,000 to $62 million in five years, and another business' revenue from $100,000 to $12 million in three years. Despite the recession, she tripled sales to $30 million at her current company.

Ana is a financial turnaround and time management expert who specializes in coaching entrepreneurs of small to medium-sized businesses.

She helps owners align their passion and values with their business goals and life dreams. Ana provides them with practical concepts and tools to apply to their money and time management issues as well as business and personal relationships.

Ana's warmth of spirit, sense of possibility and resilience are visible in her coaching, writing and relationships. She shares lessons from facets of her life and career to instruct others in achieving their own success.

oooooooooooooooooooooooo

Contact: Ana Weber
Ana@360degreesofsuccess.com
www.360Degreesofsuccess.com
Toll free: 888-416-1088
Cell: 949-422-1830

Printed in the USA
CPSIA information can be obtained
at www.ICGtesting.com
JSHW022338140824
68134JS00019B/1555